CLASS	153.89	LOCATION	
AUTHOR	CHEUNG Theresa		
TITLE	Psychic cats		

THIS BOOK IS TO BE RETURNED ON OR BEFORE THE LAST DATE STAMPED BELOW

2 4 MAY 2013 WITHDRAWN

F134

F150

F102

- 2 MAY 2017

30/11/20

D1363035

PSYCHIC CATS

PSYCHIC CATS

Theresa Cheung

CHIVERS

British Library Cataloguing in Publication Data available

This Large Print edition published by AudioGo Ltd, Bath, 2011.
Published by arrangement with Penguin Books Limited.

U.K. Hardcover ISBN 978 1 445 83726 0
U.K. Softcover ISBN 978 1 445 83727 7

Printed and bound in Great Britain by
MPG Books Group Limited

CONTENTS

Acknowledgements

Without my agent Clare Hulton's intuition and support I would not have had the opportunity to work on this delightful book and I am deeply grateful to her. Thanks also to my editor, Katy Follain, for her insight, encouragement and love of cats. I'd also like to take this opportunity to sincerely thank all the cat owners and cat lovers who contributed to this book by submitting their stories, experiences and personal thoughts to me and for allowing me to use them. I'm deeply grateful to you all, because you are the heart and soul of this book.

Special thanks to Ray, Robert and Ruthie for their love and patience while I went into exile to complete this project. Finally, thank you to the gorgeous new cats in my life—Merlin and Max—for the inspiration they gave me when writing this book and for the love and companionship they continue to give me every day. They may not be the greatest cats in the world but right now they are the greatest cats in mine.

Introduction:

The Psychic World of Cats

*I believe cats to be spirits come to earth. A cat,
I am sure could walk on a cloud without
coming through.*

Jules Verne

Cats have long been associated with magic and
mystery, but actual psychic cats? Do they
exist?

I believe that the answer to this question is a
resounding yes.

You may wonder how I can be so sure.

I'm sure because I grew up with cats and
witnessed first hand their remarkable powers.
I'm sure because of the many remarkable
stories about cats that I have come across over
the years I've been researching and writing
about the psychic world and which are
gathered together for you in this book. I'm
also sure because as soon as I was offered the
opportunity to write this book by some
wonderful synchronicity (or was it more than
that?), evidence of the psychic powers of cats
suddenly began to manifest all around me.

I've written many books on paranormal
subjects over the years but never before has
the theme of a book actually played itself out

as I was writing it. As you'll see in my first chapter, if I had any doubts before that cats might have psychic and spiritual powers two kittens—Merlin and Max—removed that doubt completely and in the process turned this book into a deeply personal project. Indeed my experience with Max and Merlin as I researched and compiled this book has strengthened my conviction that cats are psychic and spiritual animals and that a benign and often other-worldly bond most definitely exists between humans and cats. This bond has existed for thousands of years and it is so strong that it has led some people, myself included, to believe that it has no limit and may even continue after death.

The human–cat bond

The human–cat bond is all the more remarkable when you consider that, unlike dogs, cats owe obedience to no master. Typically cats are described as aloof, mysterious and independent but ask any cat lover and they will tell you what a delight and privilege it is to win the trust and subtle affection of a cat. Some even say that because it isn't easily won the human–cat bond represents the animal–human relationship at its most satisfying.

To understand the human–cat bond better it is helpful to know how that association first began and what place cats have in the animal kingdom. Like humans cats are mammals and like us they are warm-blooded, have fur or hair and rear their young on breast milk. Domestic cats belong to the family *Felidae*, which also includes the lion, tiger, jaguar, leopard, puma, cheetah, ocelot, lynx and panther. All members of the *Felidae* family have characteristics that suit them to hunting small prey: night vision, sharp claws that can retract and teeth that can tear and bodies suited to darting and leaping. The *Felidae* family is broken down into three genera, one of which is *Felis*, which contains a number of species including the domestic cat which has the species name of *catus*. Therefore the domestic cat's scientific name is *Felis catus*, regardless of breed or pedigree.

As the author of this book I make no claim to be a cat historian or cat behaviour expert but there are indications from archaeological discoveries in Cyprus, where the bones of cats and humans have been found together, that the bond between human and cat may have first been established around 8,000 years ago. It's likely that the relationship began as a practical one—because cats were used to control rodents in grain stores—but several thousand years later in 4000 bc there are signs of clear domestication in Egypt (the Egyptian word for cat was *miu*—in China it was and still is *mao*), especially in the region of the Nile

3

Delta, where there is evidence that cats were not just valued for rodent control but also as household pets. Early Phoenician travellers probably introduced Egyptian household cats to other parts of the Mediterranean on trading vessels and via overland trading routes throughout Asia, Europe and the Roman Empire. Cats can now be found all over the world, wherever there are people.

It was the rodent-killing abilities of cats which probably endeared them to humans first. By night they would hunt and kill and be rewarded by day with a comfortable place to sleep, preferably in front of a warm fire or on someone's lap or bed. Today, millions of cats all over the world living on farms, in buildings, factories and homes continue to fulfil the same role but cats have also progressed way beyond their original role as vermin destroyers. They are now highly valued for their intelligence and the soothing companionship they can give their owners as pets—if they are in the mood. Several recent studies have shown that pet owners live longer and are happier and less stressed. A cat is someone to care for other than yourself and in some instances the bond between human and cat is so powerful that the cat becomes the only thing worth living for.

Cats are also highly regarded because, whether pedigree or moggie, they are so beautiful to look at, and their aesthetic qualities have earned them a place in the art and literature of many countries. Some owners like to take things one step further and show off the beauty of their cats at shows. The first official cat show took place at Crystal Palace in the 1860s and had 170 entries, which included a tabby cat weighing 170 pounds and a newly imported 'Royal Cat of Siam' . Today many people like to breed and show pedigree cats and even make a living from it. Show cats can be long- or short-haired and are shown and judged under their respective breeds. The long-haired gene probably arose in Persia and Turkey, and the luxuriously coated Persian is probably the main long-haired breed today.

Such is the strength of the human–cat bond in the twenty-first century that there are an estimated 200 million domesticated cats worldwide, and considerable industries have sprung up to service their every need, with companies manufacturing food, toys and equipment, not to mention the countless veterinary and health care services as well as catteries, breeding homes and even cat hotels. And with the increasing tendency to confine cats for their own safety, even if only by night, a whole industry based on making sure confined cats are happy and healthy has also appeared to manufacture outdoor cat enclosures, cat flaps or indoor cat play equipment. Add to this the magazines, societies and websites devoted to cats, and the extraordinary success of *Dewey: The Small*

Town Library Cat Who Touched the World by Vicki Myron (2008) it is safe to say that our love affair with cats has never been more widespread or public.

Naturally mysterious

Just as the enduring human–cat bond dates back to ancient times, the idea that cats may be psychic or be able to see and feel things humans can't is nothing new. Perhaps the main reason cats have long been thought psychic is their elusive and independent nature. However well we think we know them, we never really do. Although they like to grace us with their company and can be incredibly affectionate, they will always remain independent and unpredictable, and this is probably why people either love or hate them. Their souls are veiled in mystery and for centuries their beauty, intelligence and independence have caught our imagination.

Read any book or article about cats and nearly always mention will be made of the fact that they were worshipped for 2,000 years as divine beings by residents of the Nile Delta. Bastet, the cat goddess, associated with protection, beauty and music, is one of the best-known deities of the ancient Egyptians' pantheon. As mentioned previously, cats were revered because they effectively saved lives by protecting food from disease-ridden rodents with their hunting prowess, but this may not have been the only reason. The ancient Egyptians may also have noticed something about cats which we often fail to in our secular and fast-paced society. As well as cats' uplifting grace and beauty they may have seen some of their healing and calming powers.

Reverence for cats can be found in many world religions. For instance, in Christianity the M marking on the forehead of tabby cats is said to be where Mary, the mother of Jesus Christ, touched and blessed a cat that comforted her baby. In Islam the M stands for the prophet Muhammad, who had a great fondness for cats. In one story, rather than disturb his sleeping cat Muezza, Muhammad cut off the sleeve of his robe which Muezza was sleeping on when the call to prayer sounded. However, alongside mention of their sacredness any discussion of cats and their mystical history will probably also mention the fact that they have also been regarded as demons.

During the medieval age cats were associated with witchcraft and regarded as witches' familiars. Some pro-cat historians have even gone so far as to suggest that the devastation brought by the bubonic plague was nature's retribution for the persecution of cats, because this allowed rodents to proliferate, and fleas on rodents were the main carriers of disease.

It's often said that cats have nine lives, and if you look at their colourful and dramatic history they have indeed managed to survive the most terrible persecution. But whether worshipped or hated, it's impossible to ignore these remarkable animals, and currently they are enjoying unprecedented popularity worldwide. In many countries cats now outrank dogs as the most popular household pet.

When you take into account the history of cats, the fact that they roam in the moonlight, have superb night vision and like to do what they please, you have many things which set cats apart as different. Set apart from the rest and mysterious, yes. But are they really psychic?

My own experience with cats makes me believe so, but first let's take a look at some pretty compelling evidence—for want of a better word.

Meet Oscar

One of the best-known examples of cats' psychic abilities in recent years is the story of Oscar the nursing-home cat. Oscar gained global media attention in 2008 when he became an uninvited guest at the bedside of residents at a care home in Rhode Island in the USA. Oscar wasn't a very friendly or beautiful cat but what made him famous was his uncanny ability to predict when a patient was going to die. Staff soon discovered that when Oscar nestled down on the bed of a patient, that person was likely to die within the next few days. Before the media got hold of the story he had accurately predicted twenty-five deaths, a number that is surely too high for it to be explained as coincidence or the lure of warm blankets.

It's certainly possible that there is a scientific explanation. Dr Joan Teno of Brown University, who is an expert on care for the terminally ill and treats people at Oscar's nursing home, has suggested that a dying person may produce a scent that cats are attracted to, but until that is proven the explanation that Oscar is a psychic cat should not be dismissed either.

Warning signs

Long before Oscar hit the headlines cats were known to have predicted natural disasters before people realized they were in any danger. In 1944 a cat called Toto lived in a town near Italy's Mount Vesuvius. According to his owner, one night Toto woke him up by repeatedly scratching his cheeks. The man got angry and tried but failed to make the cat stop. His wife recognized that the behaviour was strange and got the idea into her head that the cat was warning them about something. She convinced her husband to get up and get dressed, pack some things and get out of the area. An hour later Vesuvius erupted, burying their house and killing over thirty people.

Thirty years later, in 1975, residents of the city of Haicheng in China were evacuated due to a predicted earthquake, and one of the reasons put forward by seismologists for their prediction was the unusual behaviour of both cats and dogs. The lives of an estimated 150,000 people were saved. The same thing happened a year later in 1976 in the Friuli district of north-western Italy when people noticed that cats were behaving strangely in the early evening, running about madly, scratching at doors to get out of their houses and disappearing once outside. Around 9 p.m. a major earthquake hit the area. Similar stories have continued to be reported over the decades.

Spearheading the latest research into the phenomenon is Professor Mitsuaki Ota of Azabu University in Japan, who conducted studies on cats and came to the conclusion that some cats can reliably predict earthquakes with a seismic rating of 6.0 and above. The cats would become unsettled for no apparent reason. There are a number of explanations as to how and why cats can predict earthquakes. Perhaps they can detect underground vibrations or are sensitive to alterations in static electricity or changes in the earth's magnetic field. Some believe with their super-sonic hearing cats may even be able to hear (or is it feel?) minute magnetic chemical and sensory changes in the environment that predict what lies ahead.

It's not just natural disasters that cats seem able to predict. In World War II numerous stories circulated about cats guiding owners to safety in air raid shelters or giving life-saving warnings before the sirens wailed. All this is the stuff of legend and hard to prove as of course no scientific studies on cats were conducted, but in 1940 one cat named Faith did actually go on to earn herself a silver medal. A few days before a savage night of the London Blitz, Faith started to behave very strangely. She would hide her kitten—Panda—in the basement of a church and every time the owner brought them upstairs Faith would take herself and her kitten back down. The church was destroyed by the Luftwaffe, but brave Faith kept little Panda safe and was later discovered in the basement. Her devotion and bravery became well known throughout London, inspiring many a person through the dark days of the war.

Good for us

Perhaps even more inspiring is the very real ability of cats to be able to foresee when their owners are going to suffer seizures or other

11

illnesses. In addition to their apparent hypersensitivity to their owners' moods, feline studies have further confirmed that cats really are good for us. You'll read some remarkable stories in this book which show that not only can cats save lives, but the very presence of a cat can help relieve pain, lift spirits, lower blood pressure and aid recovery.

To those able to build a rapport with them cats can provide all these benefits and more. Building a rapport with cats may be harder than it is with dogs but it is for that reason that cat lovers find it so incredibly rewarding. Indeed for some the bond once established is so strong that the death of a cat can be as devastating as the loss of a child. As author Doris Lessing, a woman who clearly understood the beneficial power of the cat–human bond, once said, 'This was love, and for life.'

'Catnav'

Another unexplained aspect of cat behaviour, which adds a further layer to the mystery surrounding them, is their incredible homing instinct. In 2000 biologist and author Rupert Sheldrake conducted experiments in which a cat was let loose in a place he or she had never been. The cat was closely observed for its own safety, and in most cases found its way home.

One very well known case often cited as an

12

outstanding example of catnav is that of a cream-coloured Persian cat called Sugar, who in 1951 followed her family 1,500 miles from California to Oklahoma. Sugar had been left with neighbours when her owners decided that the journey might be too much of a trauma for her as she had a hip deformity. Fourteen months later a cat looking remarkably like Sugar appeared at the new home of her owners. They recognized the hip deformity and phoned their old neighbours, who confirmed that Sugar had disappeared within days of the family leaving for Oklahoma.

How did Sugar do this?

No conclusive explanation has been found for the innate navigation device that cats seem to have, but scientists have suggested that cats could have the ability to read the earth's magnetic fields, while others believe it could be down to their acute sense of smell or their ability to create mental maps of places they have visited. Opinion remains divided, but one persistent theory that also cannot be discounted is that cats have natural psychic abilities and can sense the location of their owners. Sugar's story is not an isolated one; you'll read plenty more in this book.

Naturally psychic

Even though there is scientific evidence to suggest that we are all born with an intuitive sense (which is more highly developed in some people than others), we nowadays have very little understanding, belief or trust in psychic phenomena. Nevertheless, many paranormal experts—myself included—believe that, like natural-born humans, cats are naturally psychic. In cats however this sixth sense is more highly developed than it is in us.

We all have intuition, but the difference is that cats just go ahead and act on theirs instead of questioning it as we so often do. Ask many cat owners and they will agree that their cats seem to be aware of things that we aren't and have the ability to tune into their owners' thoughts and feelings. This doesn't apply to all cats. Just like humans, cats are individuals, and some cats are more psychic or sensitive than others, but judging from the number of stories sent to me I would think that the ratio of cat owners who think their cats are psychic is fairly high. A survey done a few years ago by Cat Protection League staff revealed that just over two thirds of those who voted—around 69 per cent—via the charity's Internet site believed that cats were psychic. I've lost count of the number of stories I've heard, read or been sent over the years by people who believe their cats are psychic in the sense that they can detect when their owners are about to come home— even when the owners arrive at unpredictable times. Then there are those who truly believe that cats can sense the world of spirit and even become ghosts themselves.

Whether you believe in the paranormal abilities of cats or are cynical, there is no doubt in my mind that the vast majority of cat lovers are keen to understand more about why their cats behave as they do or are the way they are. And it is refreshing to discover a subject today that remains unexplained, isn't dismissed and still inspires heated debate. Indeed, it seems that debate about whether cats are psychic will continue ad infinitum, and all cat lovers can do is either sit on the fence or consider the evidence and decide for ourselves.

For me, the term psychic cats is an obvious one to use—if humans can be psychic why not cats, who rely more on their instincts for survival? I believe that cats definitely possess senses that we either don't have or don't see, but I hope reading this book about cats and the lives they touch will help you come to your own conclusions, or at the very least keep an open mind.

About this book

Psychic Cats is a collection of unexplained true stories about cats who demonstrate remarkable psychic powers, and 'angel cats' , felines who have refused to let death part them from their human companions. However we try to explain the often intense human–feline connection, bear in mind that cats can rarely be forced to do what they don't want to, and the stories you'll read will confirm that not only do our whiskered friends have the ability to touch our hearts long after they have purred their last, but that they can also see something in us that we can't always see in ourselves—that we can be worth comforting, loving and coming home to.

In this book I will share with you just some of the compelling stories about cats that I have collected from people whose lives have been touched, transformed and in some cases saved by cats, over the decades that I have been researching and writing features, books and encyclopedias about spirits, ghosts, dreams, angels and the psychic world. The stories you will read range from the heart-warming, humorous and inspiring to the astonishing— some may even stretch your belief—but however much they vary in content they have two things in common: they are all about cats and they are all real stories.

I'd like to begin our journey, though, with some more of my own experiences. I hope that learning a little about me and what I have learned and continue to learn from the cats I've shared my life with will help you understand my deep passion for cats and my firm belief that they may have very real psychic powers. Being a cat lover myself has given me a fantastic starting point for this book, and my work as a paranormal investigator and writer has also encouraged me to conduct my own research and draw my own conclusions about cats and their psychic abilities, many of which I will share with you throughout the book.

I also want to make it clear from the onset that I'm not a cat expert or an animal behaviour authority. I'm a forty-something mum of two children, and although I have first-hand experience of the psychic power of cats—and I hope I will continue to do so as nothing warms my heart more—I'm not a 'cat whisperer' either. I do believe, however, that there are times when we humans can tune into the psychic world of cats regardless of whether we regard ourselves as psychic or not. In other words, one thing I have discovered through personal experience and through my research and writing is that anyone can find their lives and their hearts touched by a cat.

The rest of the book explores some of the amazing cat stories that I have encountered over the twenty-five years I've been writing about the paranormal. I'm extremely grateful to all those who allowed me to talk to them and gave me permission to share their stories. A few sent me their own versions of their experiences but in most cases I have written up the stories from what I was told or sent. Everyone who contributed touched me greatly with their honesty and their respect not just for cats but for all living creatures. Although names and other personal details have frequently been changed to protect the identity of owners and the safety of the cats they describe, these true accounts from ordinary people show some of the many different ways cats can be divine messengers of inspiration, comfort and protection.

While I was writing this book many people told me that there are always perfectly rational explanations for psychic cat stories—the cat's owner may have imagined it all, for example. At first I tried to argue that this wasn't the case and would stress that the psychic powers of animals—cats in particular—have been reported for thousands of years. I would point to my own experiences and the vast number of cat stories I have gathered, and would say that in a court of law a witness statement is taken as evidence. I would argue passionately, but it often became clear that I was wasting my energy. At the end of the day it all comes down to belief, and to those who believe—either because they have a special affinity with cats or because their lives have been touched in some magical and mysterious way by them—no proof is needed. No explanation will ever have the power of their conviction that cats can see, feel and understand things we don't.

So settle down in a seat, preferably with your purring cat close beside you, and whether you have had a psychic cat experience or not prepare to be amazed and intrigued—as I never fail to be—by the true stories of people who have been astonished and inspired by the magic and mystery of cats. Working on this book has been a treat in every sense of the word and renewed my already strong belief that cats are both psychic and spiritual creatures. It is my dearest hope that reading it will serve as a catalyst to strengthen further the bond between you and your cat, or cats in general, by proving to you that cats really can and do have special powers, and that even ordinary people like you and me can wake up one day and find themselves unexpectedly invited into the mysterious but always utterly enchanting psychic world of cats.

Cat's eyes

The eyes are windows to the soul
In cats this is more so
For they see spirit all the time
Wherever a prowling they might go

Gareth Simon Gameson

1. Merlin, Max and Me

Kittens are angels with whiskers.

Author unknown

I grew up with cats as valued family members and have always worshipped them and suspected that they might have psychic abilities of some sort, so when I was given the opportunity to write this book about cats and their special powers I could not believe my luck. I looked forward to many happy hours collecting incredible stories from cat lovers and mixing them together with my own thoughts and recollections into a heart-warming recipe. After writing a number of heavy-duty encyclopedias of the psychic world the ease and contentment the project offered was irresistible. But I had underestimated the awesome psychic powers and unpredictability of cats, and their ability to turn your life and your heart completely upside down and inside out. Let me explain:

The story of Merlin, Max and me began about four years ago when my daughter started to pester me about pets. I'm sure every parent will have experienced something similar.

'Please can we have a pet? I really want a kitten or a puppy. Please, Mummy, please. I promise to look after it. I promise,'

The pestering started after my daughter— aged around five at the time—had visited a friend's house and played with a beautifully trained dog and gentle cat there. I told her that pets were a big responsibility and it might be better to wait until she was a little older. Secretly, I hoped she would forget. I grew up with a cat and would have loved for my daughter to have had one too, but right now life was just too busy for us to consider a pet. My husband was working 24/7; I had my hands full juggling numerous book projects and pulling the family together; and there were never enough hours in the day. My son was a member of many after-school clubs and I spent a lot of time running my daughter around as well. I knew that other families with young children and busy lives seemed to manage okay with pets—and I was in awe of them— but I just didn't think I could cope with someone else to look after. So for the next three years I kept putting the idea on hold. Then the pestering reached new levels of intensity when my eleven-year-old son, who had previously been silent on the topic, started to ask too.

'I want a lizard. It's not fair if she gets a kitten and I don't have anything. Please can I have a pet? I want to have a lizard. If that's not possible a snake would be cool or what about a ferret?'

Again I tried to put off the idea. I told my son that I hadn't promised his sister a kitten, ferrets weren't a good idea as they could bite and snakes could escape and kill things. I simply didn't want a lizard; it was hard to explain why. In response he spent days researching different lizard breeds and their feeding habits and cage requirements. He was like a dog with a bone, or should I say cat with a mouse. He wouldn't let it go, and every time I said no he just seemed to pester harder. He even told me he wanted to become a zoologist and it was extremely important for him to have a pet so he could study it.

'Nobody is getting a pet, especially a lizard,' I would say. 'Pets need a lot of time and attention, and we are all so busy rushing out all day and what about holidays?'

'I promise to look after it,' my son would say, echoing my daughter, 'and we don't need holidays.'

We argued backward and forwards like this for months, years. Then at the start of 2009 our family situation changed dramatically when my husband got an opportunity to retire early and reinvent himself. With a more relaxed lifestyle it somehow seemed the right time to finally treat the kids to pets. I guess we had run out of excuses. We did some research on all the children's pet ideas and decided that cats were less expensive and suited our lifestyle far better than dogs—or lizards—so at the start of the summer we told the children that instead of a holiday this year we were going to get a couple of kittens. Both my husband and I had been cat owners in the past so we knew what we were going to have to deal with. We decided to get not just one but two cats—one for my son and one for my daughter—so they could keep each other company in the day while we all went about our business. When we told the children the shrieks of joy were deafening, even from my son, who seemed to forget all about his lizard in a flash. I felt my stomach flutter with a strange kind of excitement.

Then like a bolt out of the blue literally a day or so after we had decided to get the kittens my agent called and the prospect of writing this book came up. It was remarkable. I couldn't help thinking it had to be more than just a coincidence. The timing of everything felt perfect. I have to admit I felt a little smug about it all, even wondering if some higher power, or dare I say feline force of nature, was at work encouraging me to believe in this book.

We all liked the idea of adopting kittens from either the RSPCA or Battersea Dogs and Cats home. My husband especially liked the idea as it was a much cheaper option than buying from breeders. We filled out all the necessary forms and went to visit some catteries but when the kids saw so many kittens and cats things got very complicated. My husband was particularly struck with a beautiful black kitten called Hermione. My son wanted every kitten he saw, and my daughter fell in love with a pair of five-year-old black and white cats. As for me I had no special preference. I knew that whatever type of cat we got I'd be happy because I felt at home with cats whatever their breed. I just wanted everyone to be happy.

Nobody could make a decision but eventually, after much discussion, we settled on a pair of black long-haired kittens, even though we weren't given the opportunity to touch or hold them. They were both available and we wanted to take them home straight away but were told it might be best to wait a few days because they were still recovering from a stomach bug. The next few days rushed by as eager preparations were made for the new arrivals.

On the morning we were due to pick up the kittens I woke up with a really striking image in my head. In my dream two cats were licking my hands—one was grey and black and the other was ginger and cream. They didn't look like any of the cats we had seen. We had all eventually agreed to focus our search on black kittens because they have such a hard time being rehomed due to their association with bad luck, but these dream kittens weren't black and they felt so real and alive. One of the kittens—the grey one—was particularly affectionate and his eyes were like deep pools of love and mystery.

I'm not psychic, although I have from time to time had hunches, dreams and experiences I can't explain which have on occasion turned out to be true or to offer me unexpected insights, so I did spend time reflecting on the significance of this dream. It was the dream's clarity that really struck me. I didn't know the cats, but given that I was working on this book and the fact that we were about to pick up a couple of kittens, I eventually came to the conclusion that my mind was simply preoccupied with all things feline.

When we drove to the cattery later that morning I had a strange and unsettling sense of foreboding I couldn't explain. Then, sure enough, when we arrived we were told something we hadn't been aware of before. The kittens we were due to pick up might in fact be more suited to a family without children as sadly they had been badly mistreated in the past. We could take them but were warned that they would need a lot of care and attention and even then might not become the affectionate pets my children dearly wanted. Much as we would have liked the kittens my husband and I decided not to take the risk. We simply didn't have to the time to take them on and give them the attention they deserved. We also knew how disappointed the children would be if the kittens ran away from them at every opportunity.

My daughter cried and my son sulked when they heard. I was anxious about what would happen to the kittens but was told not to worry as the cattery had another person interested in rehoming them and it was important that we found the right kittens for us. They would call us when they had any suitable arrivals. For the next few days we waited and waited but did not get the call. I tried to explain to the children that we hadn't really given things enough thought. Many rescue animals had been mistreated or were semi-feral and we were not perhaps the ideal family for them.

It was time to hit the Internet and do a search for breeders in our area. I could not believe my eyes when the first picture I downloaded was that of three twelve-week-old Persian-cross kittens, two grey and one ginger and cream. They looked strikingly like the cats I had seen in my dream. Laughing inside at the coincidence, I phoned, thinking they were so cute they had probably gone, but was delighted when I heard they were all still available, and at a very reasonable price. I asked the children and my husband if they were interested, and as soon as they saw the pictures they asked me to organize a visit.

When we went round to see the kittens the

breeder told us that just ten minutes before we arrived someone else had taken one of the grey kittens and there were only two left. The remaining grey kitten would probably not have been our natural choice as he was a lot smaller and not as pretty in his markings as the other one. Despite this he captured our hearts the moment we saw him. He came bounding over to us purring loudly, his whole body shaking. He was so tiny and made us laugh as he tumbled around with such enthusiasm. His brother was a little cooler in his welcome but still enjoyed the attention. We had no say in the matter. It's often said that cats choose their owners, and it was obvious that the cats had found their new owners, or should I say pets?

Later that evening both kittens were safely home and revelling in the warmth and cuddles we gave them. My daughter had adopted the cream and ginger one and called him Merlin while my son had adopted the tiny tearaway and called him Maximus Brutus, or Max for short.

As I watched my children play that first night with the kittens a knot disappeared from my stomach. After all the searching I felt that we could now relax and enjoy hours, days and months of cuteness and happiness with the kittens. Once again everything seemed so right. I truly believed that Merlin and Max had been calling out to me in my dream, and now I really had all the inspiration I needed to write this book. As I mentioned previously I would not describe myself as psychic, but I have on occasion experienced insightful dreams or flashes of intuition, and I wondered if owning cats again might actually be the catalyst for greater psychic awareness developing within me. It all felt so exciting, and with the pet issue finally sorted it was now time to turn my full attention to this book.

I was wrong again.

Within twenty-four hours Max was poorly and things swung from perfect to feeling like nothing was going right. We rushed Max to the vet only to be told that he had a potentially fatal condition called external rectal prolapse, which in lay person's terms means part of his colon was coming out of his body. He would need stitches immediately under general anaesthetic but there was no certainty that the condition would not reoccur or that he would survive. As Max was taken out of my arms he gave me a lingering and intense look. I knew in my heart that it was the same look that the grey kitten had given me in the dream I'd had a few days ago.

Returning home with an empty crate was unbearable. Merlin wailed for his brother and my son felt his absence keenly. I went to sleep that night and woke up with my face wet with tears. I had really looked forward to starting work on this book and now with everyone so unhappy and unsettled because of the kittens I didn't have the heart. How could I write about owners lavishing attention on their cats and the comfort and love their cats offered in return when I felt like this? I didn't think I could bear to write the book if our story didn't have a happy ending and wondered if I should delay or even cancel the project. I could not believe the feelings this little bundle of fur was arousing in me. I had gone from elated and excited to angry and wretched. I had only known Max for less than a day but he had already torn into my heart and had a hold over me that I can't explain.

The whole family waited anxiously for news of Max. At around 4 p.m. the phone rang and we were told he had made it through the operation but was very, very weak. Every day we would phone and every day we were told that there was progress but it was still touch and go. We visited him one day but in retrospect it would have been better not to as he looked pitiful and frightened the children. He had one of those collars on to stop him licking his stitches and was desperately trying to clean himself but couldn't. His bottom was sore and he slept most of the time in his litter tray. He was skeletal and filthy, but despite being in obvious pain when he saw us still hobbled forward on his tiny legs and started to purr. Not wanting to think about the days that stretched ahead, we left when he fell asleep

Several days into this it began to dawn on us how much Max's operation and ongoing care was going to cost, especially if he suffered a prolapse again and needed a costlier operation, which was a strong possibility. We had intended to insure him on his first visit to the vet for a vaccination so he wasn't yet covered. We had not anticipated that he would fall seriously ill on his first day home with us, and to make matters worse if the condition reoccurred we would never be able to claim for it as it was now a pre-existing condition. Our summer of fun with the cats was turning into a nightmare, an expensive nightmare. The practical side of me was now saying that it would be kinder to have Max put down, given the fact that he was in such obvious pain. A number of my friends told me I was mad for not returning the cat to the breeder and demanding my money back or handing him over to the RSPCA.

Finally, late one evening, with Max still not making any progress and the likelihood that his condition might reoccur and cost us yet another arm and leg, we decided to return both Max and Merlin to the breeder. We had wanted two kittens to keep each other company and knew that finding a feline friend for Merlin outside his litter might be tough, so we decided to return them both. I felt helpless and horrible about this, but tried to convince myself it was for the best.

The moment we made the decision to contact the breeder and return the kittens the normally placid Merlin changed his behaviour dramatically. My husband said it was because he missed his brother but it really was as if he knew what we were planning and was angry with us. On one occasion he scratched my arm badly and refused to touch his food. Previously he had been happy for my daughter to cuddle and fuss over him. Now he didn't want to know and tried to escape or hide at every opportunity. Was Merlin reading our minds? He even took to sleeping on top of the crate we had taken him home in as if to say, 'Well, if you are going to take me back, just do it now.'

Things were in a bad way. I was horribly behind in my work, my household chores, everything. I couldn't even contemplate beginning this book and with no time extension possible it looked increasingly like the project wasn't going to happen. I felt miserable. We were spending money we didn't have on a kitten we had had for only a day. It was all so unfair. A part of me was furious. Having a kitten should be a precious and special time full of magic and fun but it had turned into this nightmare. There was me thinking that semi-pedigree cats purchased via a breeder would sidestep the difficulties of homing kittens that had been strays or mistreated by their first owners. I'd tried to make things easy for myself and the children but I'd actually made things a hundred times worse. Now I had one kitten that hated us and another that was desperately ill, and even if he survived there was no telling how he would adjust to home life after his ordeal. I knew I was being ridiculous but I couldn't help but think I was being taught a lesson for not showing enough compassion to the kittens we had intended to rehome at Battersea before Merlin and Max came on the scene.

The children were confused and upset and I veered between compassion for the kittens and my desire to see my children happy. Sometimes I just wanted to forget about Max and Merlin and start afresh with two new kittens. My husband felt concern for Max but, like me, was worried about the cost. Everybody was distraught. I hadn't felt this helpless and depressed since my mother—a cat lover all her life—had died, and I was shocked at the intensity of emotions I was experiencing. What was going on?

Anyone reading this who isn't a cat lover may think I'm barmy getting so worked up about the life of a kitten. I agree. There are many terrible things in the world happening to humans every day, and here I was crying about a twelve-week-old kitten, but ask any cat lover and they will tell you that cats have this uncanny ability to make those who care for them lose all sense of perspective. I'm just setting down as honestly as I can how I felt.

33

Most of the time I'm actually quite a logical and rational person with the ability to stand back and look at a situation objectively, but in the weeks following Max's operation I lost all sense of perspective. It really felt as if my heart was being torn up.

One night I couldn't sleep for worry so I sat up and put my bedside lamp on, careful not to wake my husband. I reached over for a glass of water and got a shock when I saw Merlin sitting on the end of our bed. I was surprised because I hadn't heard him jump up and because before I went to bed I had fed him and, after tidying up in the kitchen, left him on some blankets there. I clearly remembered closing the door. To this day I have no idea how he got out of the kitchen and into our bedroom.

For a few moments Merlin stared at me and I stared back. As we stared I started to blink away tears and he came forward to investigate, purring more loudly than I had ever heard him purr before. Unlike his brother he had always been restrained in his displays of affection and only purred on rare occasions, so this touched me deeply, especially as for the last few days he had been so vicious when anyone approached him. Silently I told him that I was sorry I was letting him down and that we simply couldn't cope with Max's condition. He rubbed his head against my hand and then curled up beside me. It had been over twenty-five years since I had last had a cat sleep with me, and fond memories of cuddling up together at night came flooding back to me. Calmness wrapped around me like a warm blanket and I fell into a deep sleep.

In the morning I woke with a start. Light was shining through the windows and I looked down at the place where Merlin had slept. It still felt warm and there were a few stray hairs but he wasn't there. I got up and called for him but there wasn't a sound. I went downstairs and saw that the kitchen door was slightly ajar. Merlin was sitting under the kitchen table calming licking himself, and when he saw me he jumped up and arched his back with his tail held high. Again I wondered how he could have got out of the kitchen in the night without someone opening the door because I was convinced I had closed it.

I ran upstairs but everyone was still fast asleep. At breakfast I asked if anyone had got up to let Merlin out during the night but nobody knew what I was talking about. Perhaps it had been a particularly vivid dream and Merlin hadn't visited me at all. But it felt so real, and what about the stray hairs? I tried to figure out if there was a way for Merlin to have opened the door by himself but it was impossible. Somehow Merlin had visited me in the night and somehow this visit had changed everything because from then on I just knew that we all had to hang in there with Max for as long as it took. We were going to keep both the kittens in sickness and in health.

When I explained to the children that we weren't going to give Max and Merlin back they were not at all surprised; neither was my husband. Deep down I guess they all knew that none of us really had the heart to send them back, knowing that their chances of being rehomed together with one cat suffering an ongoing medical condition were poor. Looking back it was a harsh way for the children to learn that life with pets isn't always about cuteness, cuddles and fun. There is always the risk of complications and illness but the lessons they were learning were important ones.

The day after I made the decision to keep Max the vet called to say that he looked stronger than he had previously and there was finally reason for us to be optimistic as his wounds were healing. Again I couldn't help but wonder if Max had somehow sensed our change of mind and this was giving him strength to fight. It was to be another seven days before Max eventually came home and mercifully the vet's bill was not as high as we had originally thought. During this week of waiting and hoping the bond between Merlin and me grew and grew. He was also much gentler with the children and let them play with them. He didn't hiss and scratch any more. I always left the kitchen door open from now on and he continued his night-time visits. He was naturally quiet, elegant and aloof, but as the only cat in the house he began to seek out our company more and more.

Thankfully—otherwise *Psychic Cats* may well not have been written—this story does have a happy ending. Max made a full recovery, and to date there has been no sign of a relapse. I know cats purr a lot, but when he finally arrived home he literally didn't stop purring for the first twenty-four hours. In the weeks ahead he got stronger and more confident with us. Not surprisingly, after experiencing such a trauma, it wasn't easy winning Max's trust, and after the euphoria of settling in he became nervous and jumpy. We had to earn his confidence. He needed a lot of space, time and patience—and my children again learned a valuable lesson about animals needing time, tenderness and patience to bond with humans. Without realizing it I had sent my kids all the wrong messages by buying a cat on the Internet. Pedigree or not all cats need to be treated with care and love before a strong bond can be established.

After a few months Max gradually lost his fear and made his first tentative steps towards us. It was a truly wonderful moment one night when he ran into the living room and sat next to us as we all watched television. Previously, his preferred place to nap was in the drawer under my bed, but he had chosen to spend his time with us instead. We didn't fuss over him that night—although we all longed to—as we wanted him not to feel threatened. A few nights later he was lying on his back with my son and daughter stroking his tummy. With Merlin watching everything from his favourite armchair—formerly my husband's chair—my family truly felt complete.

Today it is incredibly hard to tear ourselves away from Max and we fight to cuddle and play with him. Merlin is equally adorable but still the more restrained one in his displays of affection, and when Max returned home he re-established himself in his preferred onlooker role. From time to time Merlin will deign to jump on an expectant lap and allow us to pet and cuddle him, especially if we tempt him with a sliver of cheese. I do feel that Merlin shares a special closeness with me. At times it seems he can read my mind. He doesn't like being picked up as much as Max but will tolerate it when I can't resist grabbing him because he looks so cute. If I come into a room he usually purrs for about thirty seconds by way of greeting. You could say it was my imagination but every time he purrs just for me it really feels like he is saying, 'I love you.'

The kittens have only been with us for a few months but what an impact they have had! They have helped me remember how special it is to have a cat share your life and what playful, calming and loving creatures they can be. They have triggered many fond and special memories of the first cat I ever owned, called Crystal (more about her in Chapter 2), and the love, guidance and comfort she gave me as I was growing up.

After those difficult first few weeks it's clear that from the moment they saw us that it was Max and Merlin who adopted us and not the other way around. Whenever they amble into a room to greet us it feels like a royal visit, and everybody feels so excited that they have chosen to spend time with us when they have so many other great things they could be getting on with: exploring, stalking, playing and sleeping. We gave them care and devotion during a time of crisis and I think they both know that. They are now repaying us with love, laughter and fun.

We were a happy family before but the whole experience has drawn us even closer. We spend hours watching their antics, thinking up daft games to play with them, helping them find the best places to nap and kneeling down beside them when they are in what my son and daughter call 'soppy cat mode'—usually after a play and meal, when they lie down in the sunshine or by a radiator, start purring and look at us over their stomachs with huge, sleepy eyes. When they are like that everything has to stop—chores, homework, everything. We simply have to kneel down, cuddle and worship them.

When we go out we miss them and look forward to the moment when we come back home and are welcomed by the patter of tiny feet down the stairs. It's extraordinary what a difference they have made. Looking back, even though my children were young, we were in danger of leading increasingly separate lives, but now it feels like we are a family unit again. Most of all I can't believe how much the kittens have helped me unwind. Life used to seem like an endless list of 'to dos' but Max and Merlin have really shown me the importance of relaxing, playing and 'wasting' time together as a family again.

In fact, the kittens took up so much of my time that completing this book to deadline once again became an issue. Author Dan Greenburg once said, 'Cats are dangerous companions for writers because cat watching is a near perfect method of writing avoidance.' I had no idea how true this was. Every time they did something cute—which anyone who has ever had kittens knows is pretty much all the time—I would lose all powers of concentration. Knowing that their first few weeks in our house hadn't been as warm and welcoming as they should have been, I found myself spending ages taking time to learn about them, playing with them, petting them and trying to win their trust and love. If either of them made the first move and sat close by, even if I needed to be somewhere else I'd sit absolutely still not wanting to break the magic of the moment.

Everything took twice as long as it should do when the kittens were around. Tearing myself away from them became harder and harder and I hated shutting them away in the kitchen. Eventually I decided that the only option was to give them the freedom to roam the house while I worked. It was the best idea. Hearing them bounding up and down the stairs was wonderful inspiration, and suddenly the words flowed and what had seemed a daunting task became a pleasure.

After a while I was even able to leave my office door open, and when they came to pay me a visit I felt truly honoured. Instead of making a mess, getting behind my PC or causing chaos—as might be expected—they simply came in quietly, jumped onto my desk and sat staring at me. It was as if they knew that this is the place I work, and fun and games can take place in the rest of the house. It will be interesting to see if it is just because I was writing a book about cats that they have been so well behaved and respectful. I guess I'll only know that when this book is finished and I start work on something else. All I can say is that whenever I hit a mental block during the writing of this book, nine times out of ten one or both of the kittens would be sitting on my desk looking at me as if to say, 'I'm all the inspiration you need. It's important what you

41

are doing. Now get on with it.'

Living with Max and Merlin has certainly strengthened my belief that cats have psychic powers. It has also inspired me to seek out stories from other people about their cats, and the more stories I collected the more clear it became that in many respects I was perhaps 'destined' to write this book.

I've been writing about matters paranormal for over a decade now, and since some of my titles have become best-sellers my mail box has started to swell with stories from people who believe their lives have been touched in some way by the miraculous. A significant number of these stories are about animals and top of the tree are stories about cats. For many years I simply collected these stories and filtered them into my books whenever a section on 'animal angels' or miracles was required, but then my agent called and this book became a possibility—around the same time Max and Merlin came into my life. It was also around the time that distressing reports filtered into the media about the increasing numbers of cats in need of rehoming because their owners don't believe they can afford to look after them any more in these challenging economic times. So, if this book in any small way can encourage people to welcome cats into their lives, cherish the ones they already have or respect cats for the truly amazing creatures they are, then my work will be done.

The intense closeness I now feel to cats has a lot to do with Max and Merlin, but as I pointed out earlier perhaps the most significant impact the kittens have had on my life and writing is that they brought back clear memories of my first cat, Crystal—memories of unconditional love and warmth and comfort that I should never have allowed to be buried by bouts of depression and the stresses and tensions of growing up, leaving home, establishing myself in the world of work and raising a family.

I was a toddler when Crystal became part of my life so I never really knew her as a kitten, but I did get to know her very well in the years that followed. And today, even though she died over two decades ago, it feels like I am remembering and discovering more and more about her and her enduring influence on my life and the direction it has now taken.

I'd like to tell you more about Crystal in the next chapter . . .

2. A Simple Tail

What greater gift than the love of a cat?

Charles Dickens

'Everything I need to know about life, I learned from my cat.'

I couldn't believe that these words had just come out of my mouth. I had just spent the last few hours attending a very solemn workshop on expanding your spiritual awareness and making sense of your life using meditation techniques. After a series of fairly uninspired lectures we had all been invited to contribute our thoughts. Keen to learn and grow, I had listened intently to everyone else speak wisely and sensitively about their life journey. Now it was my turn, but instead of making a sensible contribution I was talking about cats. I was quoting the first thing that had come into my mind, the title of a short feature I had read in a magazine a few days previously about cats and their laid-back approach to life. I really was losing it now.

Everyone looked at me with raised eyebrows. The workshop leader coughed and I smiled weakly back at him. I tried to explain that I wasn't trying to be disruptive. I really had had a flash of insight that made perfect sense to me, but I could tell that I was making everyone else feel uncomfortable. I quietly excused myself and left the room feeling lighter and happier than I had for years.

I've never forgotten that moment. It happened nearly twenty years ago now. It was one of those breakthrough 'ah-hah' moments when you suddenly get a sense of clarity and feel stronger than you had previously believed yourself to be. From that moment on I made the decision to follow my own path in life. I was done with workshops and seminars telling me how to live. I was going to be independent-minded, like my cat.

At the time I was seeking help in discussion groups and seminars because I was going through a particularly rough patch. I was grieving the recent death of my mother from cancer and searching for some sense of meaning and purpose in life. I'd just broken up with my boyfriend and was feeling cut up about that, and to make things worse had been made redundant from my job. In short, I was in my mid-twenties but felt that my life was ending. I was lonely, broke and scared, with no family and friends around me, so was searching for comfort and inspiration in self-help books and seminars and spiritual workshops. All too often all these things just made me feel worse.

Looking back at my diaries from those days of searching I can see that I was probably suffering from depression. Some days were better than others but most of the time I felt worthless. I felt like nothing I did really mattered. I also felt incredibly tired. Everything felt like an overwhelming task, even sometimes getting dressed or brushing my teeth. My brother, who lived abroad at the time, tried to convince me to take better care of myself, but I couldn't see the point. Along with my physical fatigue I also felt mentally tired. I had to force myself to do anything. I felt trapped, stuck in a pit of worthlessness, and I often wondered if things would ever get better. And then, when I was at my lowest ebb, like a bolt out of the blue I remembered something I should never have forgotten: the love of my cat. Somehow just when I needed them, my most fond memories of the precious hours I spent with her gave me my fighting spirit back.

All this probably doesn't make much sense, but I'm hoping it will when I tell you the story of Crystal, the cat who grew up with me.

Meet Crystal

Crystal died twenty-five years ago. It still hurts when I remember the sense of loss and emptiness when she passed away. Someone once told me, 'Grief is the price we pay for loving,' and when Crystal died the truth of that statement hit me for the first time like a hammer hitting a bruise. I had loved Crystal for eighteen years. She had been with me from childhood to adulthood, and when she passed it was hard to comprehend that she was gone. She left a hole in my heart that wouldn't go away. I felt like I wanted to throw up constantly and that I was going through the motions of my life. I wondered if the pain I felt would ever ease.

The feeling of loss and emptiness I felt at Crystal's passing was something that my friends and family at the time didn't really understand. 'She's only a cat,' they would say. They didn't understand because from as early as I can remember Crystal had been my constant companion, my loving friend. I was a lonely and withdrawn child but she had always been there and loved me no matter what, because I loved her.

I don't really have a memory of life before Crystal because she was given to me as a birthday present when I was three. I have no idea where my father got her from but I suspect she was a stray. My mother and father called her Roddy, but from the start I didn't like the name and always called her Crystal because her yellow eyes were so bright and clear like a crystal, so that's what everyone else eventually called her too.

From the very start Crystal would seek out the warmth of my bedroom at night, but much to my disappointment she didn't sleep on my bed right away. She didn't like being cuddled either. I tried many times to get her to sleep with me and sometimes she would hover uncertainly on my bed for a few moments but she always jumped off and slept on the floor or under the bed instead. Eventually I stopped trying to pick her up all the time and accepted that she preferred to be left alone. I still enjoyed her company though, and she must have enjoyed mine because she was always close by, especially when I went to bed at night. As a child I was terribly afraid of the dark and would wrap myself up tightly in my blankets. Often I would talk or sing to her and she'd watch me from a safe distance with her wise eyes. Although she didn't cuddle up to me, just knowing she was in the room with me at night was a comfort.

One particularly vivid memory stands out. I was around seven or eight years old and my mother and father were arguing again. I woke up and heard them shouting at each other in the kitchen. I hated it when they shouted as it often went on into the small hours of the night. I reached for my comfort blanket as I still couldn't sleep without it but couldn't find it. I didn't dare go downstairs to look for it because my parents might be angry with me.

Then I heard Crystal jump onto my bed. She climbed onto my chest purring heavily. Her purr was so loud that I couldn't hear the shouting any more. In that moment I felt protected and loved as never before. I didn't reach out for her because I didn't want her to jump off so I lay absolutely still enjoying the sensation of her closeness to me. It felt like I was drinking hot chocolate on a cold night. I never needed my comfort blanket after that. From then on every time I woke up scared and in need of comfort Crystal was there.

I'll never know why she chose that particular night to decide to sleep on my bed instead of the floor but it was a breakthrough because now she was always there when I went to bed. It was the beginning of a wonderful closeness between us. She would always be gone when I woke up in the morning so I don't know if she stayed all night with me or just until I was fast asleep, but going to bed wasn't a trauma any more. Until then I'd always put my head under the blankets at lights out, but with Crystal's help I learned to feel comfortable in the darkness.

In the years ahead I changed schools several times as my family was often on the move due to my mum's work as a psychic counsellor, but there was always one constant in my life— Crystal. Whenever we moved into a new house Crystal would spend a day or two sniffing everything and then she would settle down and do what she did best: play, stalk and sleep. Unconsciously I think I learned a lot from her about adaptability and making the best of whatever new situation I found myself in.

Making lasting friendships was always an issue as I was never in one place for long, but I usually fitted in well to whatever new environment I found myself in. A large part of that was probably due to the fact that I knew I could always count on Crystal to be there for me.

On one occasion we left Crystal behind when we moved. It was the year I was due to start senior or secondary school and I had had the most horrible summer. I'd been fairly happy in the school I'd been at for the last two years—a record for me—and I really didn't want to leave. I don't think Crystal wanted to leave either, because we lived beside a huge field with woods and she must have had a very exciting time. The new house was in a built-up area and I worried that she wouldn't have nearly as much fun.

On the day of the move I started to get anxious because Crystal didn't show up for breakfast. She had been with me the night before but must have left early in the morning. We didn't have a cat flap but my mum always left a window open for her. That morning, however, as my mum was getting the house ready for us to leave all the windows had been closed. She hadn't done it on purpose; she really thought Crystal was inside sleeping with me. We looked everywhere but couldn't find her.

By lunchtime Crystal still hadn't arrived. I

was sick with fear that something might have happened to her, as she had never done this before. I needed her to be with me. Moving always scared me. I couldn't bear to think of her trying to jump into the house with the windows all shut. I begged my mum for us to wait until she showed up but my mum said we couldn't and it was time to leave. She did promise, however, that we would return the next day to look for Crystal as we were only moving ten or so miles away.

Tears streamed down my face as we drove away. I couldn't settle into our new house. I just counted down the hours and the minutes until we could return and search the area for Crystal again. But we never got to return because the night we arrived my mum fell ill with a stomach bug. It was obvious she wouldn't be able to drive in the morning. I asked her if I could go by myself but she wouldn't let me because she said I was too young. My dad wasn't on the scene any more so she told me that it would have to wait until she got better. I waited for four whole days. It was torture. I knew it wasn't my mum's fault that she was ill but I had to find Crystal. My mum tried to reassure me that Crystal was a clever cat and cats were survivors and that I shouldn't fret so much. I tried to be brave and to listen to what she was saying but all I could think of was Crystal meowing for me and me not answering.

Finally, four long days later my mum told me she felt better and that she would take me back to our old house the following day to look for Crystal. I begged her to take us right away but she needed to be at work and I had to watch the hours, minutes and seconds tick away again. I remember going to bed at 6 p.m. wishing the rest of the night away so it would be morning and we could begin our search. Then the most incredible thing happened. I was drawing my curtains and I heard a meow outside my bedroom. I stood on my tiptoes and saw Crystal sitting outside. I rubbed my eyes in disbelief but she was still there. I raced downstairs and out of the front door and she trotted in with her tail high. She looked much thinner but mercifully there were no signs of injury. I don't know how she did it but Crystal had found me. It was a miracle.

Being only a child at the time I was just happy to have Crystal back. I didn't really think about what an extraordinary thing my cat had just done. How had she managed to find me?

A few years later Crystal did something else really special for me. I was about fourteen at the time and my increasingly fragile self-confidence took an even greater knock when I started at a new school again and got caught up with a crowd of girls who weren't really the friends I thought they were. Pathetically, I tried to do everything to fit in with them and make them like me. I tried to dress like them and talk like them, but the more I tried the more insecure I felt—and with good reason because I eventually found out that they had been making fun of me behind my back. I guess when your mother is a psychic counsellor it's easy to become the butt of everyone's jokes.

It's one of the worst feelings in the world when you are a teenager and your friends betray you or let you down. I cried my eyes out for a whole weekend and faked a stomach ache so I wouldn't have to go into school on Monday to face them. Those girls had been my world, and I didn't know who I was without them. I begged my mum to let me change school but she wouldn't because she had just started a new part-time job.

On the day I was due to go back to school I was terrified. I barely touched my breakfast and stumbled reluctantly out of the door. As I made my way down the road to the school bus stop I felt something brush against my legs and could not believe my eyes when I saw that it was Crystal. Since her disappearance when we had moved house and she had found me she had rarely ventured far from home, especially near to the busy main road. She hated traffic so her coming out with me like this was unusual. I didn't want to risk losing Crystal again so I bent down to pick her up and ran home with her in my arms. I gave her to my mother and then dashed back, only just catching the bus.

I don't know if it was the endorphin effect of the running or the fact that Crystal had shown me that she could be courageous too by venturing out of her comfort zone, but going back to school that day wasn't nearly as bad as I thought it would be. Knowing that my so-called friends couldn't be relied on, I stopped trying to hang out with them and concentrated on my studies instead. I figured it was better to be alone than to be with people who made you feel worthless. It took a while but eventually I found a couple of friends who liked the real me. I didn't feel the need to impress them or be someone I wasn't any more.

Over the next few years Crystal continued to work her magic in my life without me even realizing it. Looking back, I think the most important lessons I learned from spending so much time with her came from her independence and her subtle assertiveness. Crystal would never do anything she didn't want to. She had a routine but she was also unpredictable at times. She expected and usually got my undivided attention. Her meow always made me jump, teaching me not to be afraid to speak up and ask for what I want or be what I want. Her grace and dignity showed me the importance of good manners at all times. She also taught me not to allow a beautiful day to pass without savouring the moments of joy that can be sucked out it. Above all, though, she taught me about giving unconditional love and receiving it in return, and using my intuition to understand things about myself, others and the situations I found myself in.

Many of the cat owners I spoke to during the course of writing this book agreed with me that their cats have taught them many valuable life lessons, and later in the book I will share with you some of the wonderful insights they have shared with me. Sadly, it wasn't until after Crystal had died and I had the insight of an adult that I was to fully understand the true value of the life lessons she taught me, but the seeds were sown, just waiting for me to rediscover them and surprise everyone, including myself, nearly ten years later in a spiritual awareness workshop.

As I walked away from that workshop it really felt as if a weight had lifted off my shoulders. There was a way to go yet and it would take many years to build my self-confidence and find my true path in life, but I knew at that moment that I would never feel quite so useless and confused again. Memories of Crystal and the devotion she had given me reminded me that I wasn't worthless. I was worth loving and coming home to; I was worth finding and I was worth comforting; and, as you'll see below, I was even worth crossing the boundary between this world and the next for.

I've fast-forwarded a bit here so need to take you back to the final years of Crystal's time on earth, where once again her influence on my life and the direction it would eventually take was to prove to be extraordinary.

One final goodbye

If you had told me twenty-five years ago that I would one day write a book that featured stories about psychic cats and cats that have visited their owners from beyond the grave, I would have found it very hard to believe. Although I grew up in a family of spiritualists and psychics and have been fascinated by the supernatural all my life, in my childhood and early adult life I never actually experienced any personal evidence of the existence of a psychic or spirit world, animal or otherwise. I didn't levitate in my cot, talk to animals or see dead people in the playground, and I certainly couldn't read anyone's mind. I often couldn't tell the difference between intuition and my imagination or fear. I did have vivid and colourful dreams but they were never precognitive. In fact, I was very normal—if there is such a thing. I had a lot of anecdotal evidence of the supernatural from the people I loved and trusted but I had not inherited the 'gift' .

If truth be told, a part of me was relieved that I didn't have psychic powers because witnessing them manifest in members of my family frightened me. Like many people, I was content to simply observe, rather than experience the psychic world first hand. Then one night at the age of twenty my world view shifted subtly when for a brief moment Crystal returned to me and I received a fantastic paranormal gift.

Crystal died two weeks before I was due to leave home for the first time to study at university. Just getting into university was a massive shock for me and my family because nobody, myself included, thought it was possible. Because we were always on the move I left school at sixteen with a very poor batch of results. Then I got a job working as a care assistant in an old people's home. I still wanted to study and learn though, so I decided to do some A levels via correspondence. It was a tough and isolated way to study and I often wondered if I was up to the task but things always seemed easier when Crystal came into my room purring loudly. She would sit with me and when I felt low it was so reassuring to reach out and hug her. I honestly don't think I could have done it without her. Nobody, especially me, could believe it when my results came through and they were good enough to get me an interview and a place at Cambridge. People asked me what my secret was, and I'd reply that I'd recommend studying with a cat by your side.

After the euphoria had died down and the reality hit me that it was time to leave home, I was very nervous about this new phase in my life and a little frightened. I'd lived a very sheltered, strange life compared to other people my age—not to mention the lack of money—and this was a huge step. I was so frightened that I thought about turning my place down and staying at home, but then two weeks before I was due to start Crystal died.

Crystal's death somehow seemed like a sign, a spur, that it was time to move on. She had been my constant companion all those years and now that I was ready to spread my wings it was as if her task on earth was done. Her passing was mercifully quick and sudden. She was hit by a car. I don't know how it happened because I wasn't there to witness it. To this day I don't understand why she ran into the road. She had a terrible fear of cars and motor-bikes and usually stayed away from roads, but I came home one day and my mum was sobbing uncontrollably, holding Crystal's limp body.

In the first few weeks at university I was terribly homesick. I missed Crystal more than I could have imagined. While living to the age of eighteen is pretty good going for a cat I couldn't get the idea out of my head that she might still have been alive if I had not been out the afternoon she was run over. I would often wake up in the night crying and I would doze off convinced that Crystal was snuggling close to me, padding the blankets as she always used to. I remember one night being absolutely sure she was in bed with me. I switched on the light, and when I looked down there was a football-sized dent on the bed where I had felt her. (And no, before you jump to conclusions, there wasn't anyone else with me at the time!)

Initially I dismissed Crystal's nocturnal visit as wishful thinking but when it happened again the following night I knew that something very real was happening. I had just climbed into bed when I heard Crystal's reassuring purr and felt the brush of her whiskers across my cheek. Then I felt little paws padding on my stomach before they settled in the spot Crystal always used to sleep. I felt the weight of her body pressing against me even though when I glanced down there was no cat there. I didn't want to move a muscle because I didn't want the sensation to end.

The next morning there was no sign that Crystal had visited me but I knew that she had come back to offer me closure and comfort when I needed it the most. I didn't mention this to anyone except my mum, who I knew was the only one who would believe me. Everyone else would have laughed in my face. For a while I questioned what I had actually experienced. I couldn't believe it was possible.

It would take several years for me to fully accept the experience for what it was, but it would eventually trigger a lot of changes in my thinking and in my life. Try as I might to explain it away, there was no getting away from the fact that I had most definitely experienced something I couldn't explain which suggested that there might be some kind of afterlife. It was the start of a lifetime of research into the paranormal and investigation into evidence of life after death. It was also the beginning of my never-ending quest to gather stories from people all over the world who believe their lives have been touched by the miraculous in some way, whether that be a life-changing coincidence, a visitation from the world of spirit, a full-blown angel sighting or the unconditional love of a pet.

All those years ago I thought my encounter with Crystal in spirit was unique, but when I actually started researching and writing books about the psychic world and my mail box filled with letters from readers keen to share their experiences, I began to realize that my experience was far from unique. Many people who have lost beloved pets believe that they have returned to say goodbye. This was confirmed again when I started writing this particular book. The number of people who have owned cats and have had experiences very similar to mine surprised me, and I take a lot of surprising given the line of work I am in.

Psychic cats or cats with an unexplained sixth sense is a concept I thought people would respond well to as many cat owners feel a strong bond with their pet, but when it came to 'spirit' or 'angel' cats I expected people to laugh or sneer. Instead I frequently got quite the opposite reaction: 'I swear my cat came back' or 'I've seen my cat's ghost.' Both the number and range of people who responded when I opened up a psychic animal email correspondence astonished and delighted me. I spoke to people from all walks of life and all were prepared to speak openly to me about their experiences.

Crystal clear

It wasn't until I started writing this book and putting into words my memories of Crystal that the full extent of her influence over me all these years later became clear. Not only did she give me perhaps my first paranormal experience and set me up for a lifetime of work and research, but she was also my constant companion, guide and educator as I grew up.

Working on this book has triggered so many memories about her that never should have been buried in the business and bustle of my daily life with children, family and work. And now as I watch my children build what I hope will be a unique and special bond with Max and Merlin—the new cats in my life—I will do all I can to make sure they remember and treasure for ever the time they are lucky enough to share with these amazing creatures.

There's so much more I could write about Crystal but I just hope that reading about the years I spent with her and what a major influence she has had—and continues to have—on my life and my writing will give you a better idea of where I'm coming from before I open up my case files. I hope you will be as moved, astonished, amused, surprised, educated and delighted as I was by the true stories reported in this book about the mysteries and marvels of the cats that share our lives in such a smooth and rewarding way and the messages of comfort, beauty, grace and hope they bring.

Before we move on I would like to invite you to reflect a moment on your own life and share with me some of your own stories about cats, or indeed any pet or animal that has touched and transformed your life in some way. (Details about how to do this can be found at the front of the book.) Who knows, your story might appear in a future book. The more we share stories about animals and how they can teach us about love and the world of spirit, or change us in unexpected ways, the more food for thought we give everyone who has ever questioned their place and value in the larger scheme of things, both in this life and the next.

3. Paws for Thought

Cats are absolute individuals, with their own
ideas about everything, including the people
they own.

John Dingman

Just the other day a friend of mine told me
that she was going to choose a cat. I was
delighted for her and told her I thought she
had made the best of decisions. What I didn't
tell her—because I wanted her to discover the
joy of this for herself—was that it wasn't going
to be her doing the choosing.

If you're a cat owner, you'll probably know
that your cat chooses you and not the other
way round. I've often heard people say this,
but I didn't really get it until I set eyes on
Merlin and Max, the cats I own today. My first
cat, Crystal, had been a gift from my parents,
and I was far too young to figure out the
'human pet' concept for myself. But years later
when it came to choosing kittens for my family
one look into their eyes and there was no
going back.

Some people make the decision to own a cat
and then go to a breeder or shelter and chose
exactly the cat they want, but for the vast
majority it does seem that the cat does the
choosing. Perhaps the kitten or cat stares at

you from the cage and it's impossible to tear yourself away, even if he or she is a long-haired cat and you were looking for a short-haired. Maybe a cat reaches out a paw or meows in your direction, and without understanding why, because you had come in search of a kitten not a cat, you are head over heels in love. Or perhaps a cat simply appears one night outside your back door and after you feed him once refuses to go away. Yes, for many cat owners it really does seem as if their cat knows exactly where it wants to be and who it wants to be with.

I suspect that cats can sense who is going to love and care for them the best, and as the following stories illustrate I also believe that the best cat–owner relationships come when we stop looking with our eyes and choose with our hearts. This first story was sent to me a few years ago by John, a man who didn't even know he was a cat person until it was too late.

TWO YEARS, SEVEN DAYS AND COUNTING

I didn't know I was getting a cat until I met my girlfriend of the time, Sarah. She really wanted a pet so I decided to buy her a puppy. What a disaster! The puppy was gorgeous but as soon as I brought him home he started to chew his way through everything. He wasn't trained either and fouled all over our flat. I really hadn't thought this pet thing through. My girlfriend was stressed and I felt out of my depth. So reluctantly we returned the dog to the breeder, who fortunately found him a good home, with a couple who actually knew something about dogs.

Despite the false start my girlfriend still wanted a pet, so a month later she came home with the tiniest tabby kitten I had ever seen. I've never really cared that much for cats but my girlfriend seemed happy, so I was happy. Despite her best efforts to win the kitten over, however, the little thing was very shy and timid. She spent most of her time under our bed, only coming out for food and to use her litter tray before scuttling back in again. My girlfriend soon grew tired of trying to coax her out and then sadly around the same time she also grew tired of me. I don't want to go into the details but we started to argue more and more about petty, silly things and eventually she moved out of my flat and my life, leaving the kitten—we hadn't even given her a name—behind.

The first night after my girlfriend walked out on me the flat seemed eerily quiet. I wasn't nearly as upset as I thought I might be. I'm quite philosophical about a lot of things, you see. Sarah and me just weren't meant to be. I flopped down in front of the television and must have drifted off to sleep. When I woke up the kitten was sitting on the carpet right close to my legs, staring up at me. I realized that I had forgotten to feed her so I went into the kitchen and gave her a bowl of food and some water. Then I returned to the TV. A few minutes later she padded back into the room and for the first time perhaps because there was a place on the sofa free jumped onto the sofa beside me, purring loudly. It was a very happy moment and totally unexpected. I was in love instantly. I shouldn't have been, as I reminded myself that this was my girlfriend's pet and she might call any day to take her back, but it didn't matter—I was in love and that was that.

My ex never wanted the cat back and in the months ahead the cat—still without a name—became very close to me. In some ways she was like a puppy in that she would follow me around everywhere. At night she would curl up in bed beside me. She had clearly decided that I was hers.

When she was about six months old I named her Cola, for the totally unoriginal reason that I'd been drinking a cola that first night she jumped up beside me. Today she is a beautiful two-year-old and a very important part of my life. Sometimes she will stare at me intently and then run up to me and when I bend down lick my fingers.

I don't know what this means, as often she doesn't want food, but I get the feeling she is happy with her choice of owner.

That's pretty much it. I've belonged to Cola for two years, seven days and counting now. There is one more thing I want to tell you though, and I find it hysterical. I started dating someone else about six months ago, and when the two of us are lying down together Cola will often crawl between us and lie down on my neck staring at my girlfriend as if to say, 'Back off. He's mine!' I find it so funny. Not sure my girlfriend does though. She's going to have to see the funny side though, as I'm just waiting for the right moment to tell her that if she wants to share her life with me she going to have to get along with Cola too!

John's story is a delightful example of a cat's ability to sense a person will really will be there for them and see more in them than a cute ball of fluff. Often this person doesn't even realize that there is a dormant cat-loving gene inside them until the cat finds exactly the right moment to activate it.

I've spoken to dozens of people like John who have told me that they didn't give cats much thought or even like them until that special cat turned up one day and wouldn't leave until it had found a home in its new owner's heart. Here's Linda's story.

CHANGE OF PLAN

I had no intention of sharing my life with a cat. My ex-husband had a cat allergy and I had been told lots of grisly stories about them—they brought in half-dead animals, they coughed up hairballs and they were only interested in people who fed them. This is how it all started for me.

I was driving home one night and I saw a couple of kids run away from the bins outside my house. I parked my car and took a look around. I couldn't see anything out of the ordinary so started to fumble for my door keys. Then I heard the faintest of mewing. It seemed to be coming from a dustbin. I looked inside and saw a kitten circling around inside. As I said I'm no cat lover, but I can't abide cruelty of any kind, especially against innocent animals who can't defend themselves, so I reached down into the bin and pulled the kitten out. The little mite was freezing cold and obviously starving. I held it up to my chest to warm it and at that moment it pressed a paw onto my chin. My life was never the same after that. This little kitten fired up so much love in me. Not only did I take the kitten into my heart and into my home, the wonderful love and companionship she gives me promoted me to devote some of my spare time to volunteering at my local RSPCA.

As Linda's experience shows, cats have this seemingly other-worldly ability to turn hearts and minds and change lives in an instant, and it all starts the moment they decide you are the one. Grace, whose story follows below, wholeheartedly agrees that when it comes to choosing a cat, the decision is often out of the owner's hands.

OVERWHELMED

When I went to visit a local breeder in her house to choose a kitten I felt overwhelmed. I wanted them all. They were just adorable. I couldn't choose. The cats were pure-breed Himalayans. It was clear that the breeder wanted me to take the remaining female grey and I was happy to have the decision made for me until I saw that there was another kitten I hadn't seen crouching in a corner all alone, away from his brothers and sister. He had brilliant blue eyes and they got very wide when I came closer to take a look at him. It was obvious that he was uncomfortable with attention. He let me pick him up though, and I knew then that he was going to be mine. Can't explain why, it was just gut instinct. I filled out the paperwork and paid the money and left the breeder with the kitten tucked in my jacket. When I got home I put him down and he followed me everywhere I went. I'm sure most cat owners say the same but I really believe I have the most adorable and precious cat in the world, that's why I've called him Precious.

Many owners like Grace have fond memories of the moment they fell in love with their cats. And if you have had a similar experience of being chosen you'll know, as Dave describes so well below, that it can often feel as if you've been given a royal seal of approval.

LOYAL SUBJECT

There's a non-smoking policy in the house I rent so most nights I'd be on my porch having a quiet smoke. One night this stray short-haired black cat comes right up to me. I recognized him. He' d been around a few years now but he'd never come this close before. He clearly had had a rough life. We looked at each other for a while and then I thought he looked in need of a good meal so I went inside and brought some chicken out to give him. He devoured it and disappeared soon after.

70

About one or two weeks later he came up to me again. This time he was wheezing and it looked like he had lost a lot of fur. I couldn't let him stay outside as it was freezing so I invited him in and he slept in the hall. The next morning I took him to the vet and this is when his reign officially began. He now spends his time hardly venturing outside and keeping me his loyal subject firmly in line. Somehow, and don't ask me why, I had expected this.

In some cases it seems that a cat doesn't choose its owner immediately. As Georgina discovered, sometimes owners need to prove themselves worthy first, and not everyone has what it takes to be a cat person:

CAT PERSON?

Cats are so unpredictable. They defy all the rules. I think my story will illustrate this well and I also hope it will help other people who sometimes think their cats don't like them.

After my first cat, Lucy, died I just knew that life wouldn't feel right until I found a feline to share it with again. I wasn't trying to replace Lucy, I just missed having a cat as beautiful and as loving as her around, so about six months after she died I bought Cosima, a stunning Persian. I bought her when she was about four months old. I expected our early months together to be a time of gradual bonding but a year down the line and I started to think she didn't like me. She only seemed to want me around when it was time to eat. If I tried to pet her she just growled or hissed. When I tried to play with her she just seemed bored and uninterested. She also started to urinate outside her litter box, gobble her food messily and rip at furniture. I couldn't understand what I was doing wrong. I bought her the best food, gave her toys and a warm bed and she didn't want to know. At times I was ready to get rid of her. She seemed so ungrateful and grumpy.

Eventually I decided to get some advice from an old friend of mine who owns not one but seven cats, yes seven. (I've read somewhere that some people are addicted to cats and I suspect she might be one of them.) When I phoned up and told her I was thinking of getting rid of Cosima because we weren't bonding she gave it to me straight. First of all she told me that all cats were individuals and I should not be treating Cosima in exactly the same way I treated Lucy. Then she told me to move slowly and speak gently around her. I'm a schoolteacher so I spend a lot of my day shouting at kids, and if you asked anyone who knew me to describe me one of the first things they would say is 'loud' . My friend told me that Lucy had been a very confident cat and had not been fazed by my loudness and quick movements but perhaps it was unsettling to Cosima. Finally, my friend suggested that I spend more time on my hands and knees, interacting with Cosima on her level. Then, if all that failed, my friend suggesting getting another cat to keep her company, as Cosima might simply be lonely.

I appreciated my friend's advice but found some of it hard to take as I'd always considered myself a cat person, but perhaps I wasn't and had just been incredibly lucky with Lucy. Anyway I thought it was worth a try as I'd invested a lot of time, money and energy into Cosima and I'm not a quitter. I couldn't believe it. After only a few days of taking her advice Cosima mellowed considerably. I could sense that the relationship between us was changing for the better.

Every night I spent about twenty minutes sitting on the floor playing with her. I'd use treats to encourage her to come to me and then when she was close I would very gently stroke her and talk to her. If she got scared or wanted to go I didn't grab or pull her back as I would have done in the past; I let her go and then a few minutes later tempted her back with some more treats.

Then one night when we were playing on the floor together Cosima walked a few feet from me, turned around and lay down. Then she looked me straight in the eyes and I saw a look there I had never seen before. I can't really describe it but the eye contact was beautiful. She wasn't frightened or angry at all and she didn't take her eyes off mine. She had never done that before. Then she got up, walked over to me and touched her nose to mine. She had never done that before. It was amazing.

I guess I just expected Cosima to be exactly the same as Lucy, but of course she wouldn't be because she is a different cat and all cats are different. I'm learning how to be a cat person with Cosima and a lot of my friends have noticed a positive change in me. They tell me I'm a lot more patient and gentle these days. It's having a knock-on effect in the classroom too as the quieter children are starting to open up to me more. It's taking a lot of time and patience but I'm getting there and it's a great feeling.

Joan went for a more direct approach when her tabby cat, Blake, didn't seem to be bonding with her.

I would describe myself as a cat person. I believe that cats just know who they like and I'm one of those people they are going to like. I've owned many cats in my life, some of them so aloof that I considered rehoming them, but then I figured they live in my house and it's my responsibility to take care of them, however unpleasant they end up. I had one cat, called Blake, that didn't seem to like me at all. He would hiss when I came near him. It was an extremely busy period in my life and I didn't have time for the softly-softly approach so I decided to show him that if he wanted to live with me he was going to be petted. I've got high blood pressure and his job was to help to lower it. So before I fed him I would pick him up, sit down with him and pet him. I wouldn't let him go until I'd had enough, and if he tried to get away he wouldn't get fed. Cats are intelligent and it didn't take him long to figure out that if he wanted to get fed he was going to have to put up with the petting. After a year or so of this—yup, you're reading this right, a year or so, it took me that long—he had fallen in love with me and was the sweetest-natured cat, happy to be petted not just at meal times, but any time.

It can be incredibly disappointing when a cat you are prepared to open your door, your life and your heart to doesn't seem to return the love you are offering with equal enthusiasm, but the overwhelming majority of cat owners I've spoken to who have experienced this say that with patience, determination and a few tried and tested techniques you can win over even the most withdrawn and timid cat. Sometimes if a cat has been badly mistreated it can be harder to overcome its negative programming towards humans and it will always remain a little reluctant to be picked up and petted, but as Roxanne's story shows it is still possible to create a deep and affectionate bond.

SO REWARDING

I got my cat when she was five years old. I got her from a rescue centre after they had patched up her broken legs. She had been really badly treated. For the first ten months she was terrified of me and would just appear when it was time to be fed. Then she would disappear and not emerge again until the next feed. I've now had her for nearly three years and she has gradually grown to see me as her protector. I did not expect her to become affectionate after what she had been through with her previous owners but she is very loving and even makes those lovely chirruping noises at me to talk.

It is so rewarding to see her grow like this but it did take a lot of time and patience. You can't make a cat like you; they're very independent but in the great majority of cases I think you can create mutual respect and trust because the bond between human and cat is a powerful and in my mind natural one. Treat a cat with love and respect and they will repay you. But bear in mind that not all cats are cuddly—I still can't pick mine up and she never sits on my lap. I have just learned to appreciate the love she does give me.

It's often said that the best way to get a cat to like you is to ignore it, but as the stories above show, if you want to create a lasting and deep bond with your cat this may not always be the best advice. We all know how well cats can hide if they want to, so if your cat makes its presence known to you this is a sure-fire sign that it wants to bond with you. Notice that they are there. Light up when they walk into a room you are in. Say their name when you notice they are looking at you. Welcome them into your life.

The bond between owner and cat is such a rewarding one that it is certainly worth fighting for, but—to return to the theme of this chapter—in many instances it really does seem to arrive immediately. There isn't any explanation for this but both owner and cat seem to know they are destined for each other. And as Sarah's story below shows, once that instant connection is made it can sometimes survive the unlikeliest odds against it.

TO THE STARS AND BACK

This happened about five years ago when I was eighteen and every time I think of it I smile inside. Mum and Dad decided to adopt a kitten from the RSPCA as a present for me. There was this tiny little tortoiseshell kitten in the first cage and he was staring at me with such friendliness as if he knew me already. I asked if I could go into the enclosure and pick him up. I told my mum and dad that this was the kitten I wanted and we didn't need to look at any more but they wanted me to have a look at all the rest. Patiently I looked at all the rest and at last they asked me what I thought. I told them what I had told them right at the beginning—that I wanted the tortoiseshell kitten playing on his own in the first cage. I had already thought of a name—Star— because I just knew I would love him to the stars and back.

We completed all the forms that needed to be filled out and then the RSPCA said they needed to do a home check before we could take the kitten home. The visit was scheduled two days later but the day of the visit came and went and nobody arrived. We drove to the RSPCA and got some horrible news. Star had died. We were asked if we would like to consider adopting another cat but I was so upset that my mum and dad decided it might be best if we let things be for a while.

Four months later we got a call from the RSPCA saying they had another tortoiseshell kitten that we might be interested in. The kitten had been adopted but had been returned to the centre. The kitten was ours if we wanted him and passed the home inspection. It still hurt that I hadn't been able to get the kitten I first chose but I told Mum and Dad I was willing to give this a try. Needless to say we passed the home inspection. Then the next morning Mum and Dad presented me with a very shy but extremely curious kitten. I called him Tool.

Within a few weeks Tool had firmly established himself as the only man in my life—apart from my dad of course. He was brilliant and I loved him deeply. In fact it became so clear that he was my cat that when I left home a year or so later when I was nineteen he came with me. It was a huge wrench leaving home and I don't think I could have coped without the love and companionship Tool gave—and continues to give—me.

I haven't got to the really special part of my story yet and that happened about three months after Tool had arrived. We were so happy with him that we asked the RSPCA to give us the details of his previous owner to thank him or her for doing the right thing and not abandoning him on the streets but returning him to the RSPCA for rehoming. It was then that we discovered something shocking and wonderful—Tool was Star. The previous owner had adopted him a few hours after we had visited the RSPCA for the first time. He had seen him and booked him the previous week so we should never have been promised him by the volunteers on duty that day as he wasn't ours to take. That's why he was in the first cage on his own—he had been waiting for collection. A series of unexplained administrative errors must then have followed including the incorrect information that he had died. The previous owner told me he had been forced to return him because his girlfriend had fallen pregnant and didn't want to share her pregnancy with a cat.

I toyed with the idea of complaining to the RSPCA but they do so much good work I can allow them this mistake and I am just so grateful that Star managed to find me again, against the odds. I often ask myself if Star chose me that day when we stared at each other for the first time. Did he know he would be returned to the RSPCA and be rehomed with me? Did he know that I was there all the time, waiting for him? My friends laugh at me when I tell them I believe we were destined for each other but in my heart I feel it to be true.

Like Sarah, Nia is convinced that her cat somehow chose her. Here's her story.

THE ONE FOR ME

I was devastated when I lost my beautiful Siamese cat Cleo. She was only twelve years old and I cried for weeks. I tried to move on but I couldn't. Coming home was a depressingly empty experience and I kept finding stray hairs and whiskers everywhere. I just knew I needed to own another cat but I wanted another cream-point Siamese, just like my Cleo.

I started to search the Internet every day but none of the pictures that came up spoke to me until I saw this stunning four-month-old cream-point Siamese that could have been Cleo's sister. I just had to have her. She was the one, so I phoned up to ask about availability. Unfortunately I was told that she was no longer available. I couldn't bear it. After all this searching I had found exactly what I was looking for and now it wasn't mine. It didn't stop me searching though, and two months later my heart nearly stopped when I saw her again. I could not believe it. I phoned up again and was told that this time she was available and I could come and see her that very day. I had to be quick though as there were a few other people interested in her.

I grabbed my car keys and raced to the owner as soon as I could. I was so scared that she might be gone when I arrived. When I came in I saw her sitting quietly and sadly in a crate. I knelt down and she immediately came up and licked my fingers and meowed. I had to hold her, so I asked if I could, and when I picked her up she purred so loudly. I told the owner that I wanted her and would fill out the forms and pay in cash there and then. I asked the owner why she had been returned and it turned out that the previous buyers had insisted on her being spayed before they collected her. After the operation they had taken her home but returned her within two weeks because they had decided she was too noisy and they didn't want to take on a Siamese any more. I couldn't have been happier that they had made this decision. I loved Angel—I called her that because she is an angel to me—from the first moment I saw her.

About ten or so days after I brought Angel home I got a speeding fine and three points on my licence and traced it back to the day that I had rushed over to get her. Under any other circumstances I would have cursed my stupidity and ill fortune for being caught by a speed camera for going just a few miles over the limit, but this time I really didn't care. It was money well spent as there was no way I was going to let Angel slip through my fingers again.

Sarah and Nia are not alone in their belief that your heart will lead you to the cat that is perfect (if you'll excuse the pun) for you. Whether it's love at first sight or a love that develops slowly and gradually with time, patience and the sharing of lives, every relationship between a cat and its owner is special, but one thing that has become clear to me from the many stories I've heard and read is that in many cases it is the cat that makes the final decision about whether or not it going to get along with its owner. Until then everyone is on probation, as Siamese breeder Sam so eloquently wrote to tell me.

In my opinion not just Siamese cats but all cats are highly intelligent. They will pick and choose who is right for them. On many occasions I think I have found lovely owners for a cat—with the right home environment and the right cat-orientated approach and often with experience of Siamese cats—but for some reason or other the cat does not settle in well. They are not bad people and they treat the cat well, but the cat just doesn't get along with them. When this happens the cat is returned to us, we rehome him and he transforms into the all-singing, all-dancing party cat we knew he could be.

Only last week this happened. I had sold a gorgeous fun-loving girl to a couple who adored Siamese cats and had this amazing house—almost a mansion—in the country, but she acted up terribly. She came back to us two weeks later and I ended up selling her to this guy who had recently divorced his wife and lived in an apartment. He'd never owned Siamese cats before so I wasn't sure it would work out but I thought I would give him a chance. A week later he phoned me up to say that she was behaving beautifully and that he couldn't be happier with his new cat.

You may think I'm a nutty cat lady if you

like, but I think if a cat doesn't like a person they will not behave very well and it won't work out. I definitely think a cat chooses its owner. I've seen this happen just too many times now.

Like Sam I've heard and read far too many stories about cats choosing their owners to dismiss them as wishful thinking. And even if you don't think this is what has happened to you, the fact that your cat is with you right now and comfortable in your presence suggests that you've been chosen without even realizing it. Cats are so independent-minded and such experts at hiding that if they didn't want you to see them you won't.

Once your cat has chosen you this is when the magic really starts. Many cat owners believe that when a firm bond is established their cat can somehow sense their moods or read their thoughts. It has always felt that way for me for all the cats I've owned and own now. We'll discuss this phenomenon in more detail in the next chapter, which explores stories of cats who appear to watch over their humans in sickness and in health, but for now whether you feel that your cat has a telepathic link to you or not the following batch of loosely connected true stories should give you plenty of 'paws for thought' . Let's begin with Amelia's fascinating experience, explained in her own words below.

One weekend I went away with my husband to visit friends in Scotland. We don't go away much longer than that because I don't want to leave Sophia, my gorgeous rag-doll cat. She hadn't been very well treated by her previous owners when she came to us and she is very timid with everyone except for us. That's why a kennel just wouldn't work as we worry that she might die from the shock. So we leave her with plenty of food in an automatic cat food dispenser that releases food every few hours and lots of water. We shut the cat flap and leave her window shelves and space to climb in. She is always a bit tetchy with us when we come home but it doesn't take long for her to settle down.

On the second and final night of our trip I had this dream about Sophia. In it she was locked in a cage and couldn't get out. When I woke up I told my husband and he said he had also had a dream about cats the previous night. He had dreamt about a litter of kittens whose mother had been killed and they were starving. We hadn't talked much about Sophia on our trip or read a book about cats or seen a movie about cats so we dismissed it as a strange coincidence.

When we got home we saw that all the food left for Sophia in the automatic timer hadn't been touched. The litter box also looked too clean. Panicking we searched the house and found that she had somehow shut herself up in the living room and had been without food and drink and her litter box for nearly three days. She must have been playing behind the door and closed it accidentally. Throughout our weekend away she had been trapped all the time and we both couldn't help thinking that she had called out to us in our dreams. Either that or we had picked up on her 'I'm hungry and alone' vibes. We felt terrible and the next morning bought some really heavy door stops so this would never happen again.

Stories about cats calling out to their owners in dreams are not as uncommon as you might think. Lucy certainly believes that Monty sent her a special dream message.

SPECIAL TO ME

I've owned many cats in my life and they have all been special to me but there is one that I think I probably loved or bonded with the most. Her name was Charm. She was a beautiful short-haired greyish-coloured cat I rescued from Battersea. The reason I got her was that I had this strange dream that I was going to find a cat that looked exactly like her. It's hard to describe if you haven't experienced it yourself but from the moment I got her I felt that she already knew me. It was like we were old friends even though we had only just met. There was just this great rapport. I loved every part of her from the tips of her ears to the tip of her tail. She even fixed me up with my fiancé.

I had this dream that she had been hit by a car. In the morning when she didn't come for her breakfast I started to feel anxious, not because she had missed her breakfast—as she had done that a few times before—but because of my dream. I ran outside and found her a few blocks away sitting beside this injured cat. The cat hadn't been hit by a car but he had his foot caught in a grate and it looked like it was broken. I took him straight to the vet, who was able to locate the owner via the cat's microchip. Yup, you guessed it. The owner called me up to say thank you and we ended up chatting for hours and eleven months later we got engaged.

Maria also believes that her cat called out to her in her dreams.

I was so excited about my trip to Thailand. I was going for a whole month. The only thing that made me feel a little sad was that I would have to leave my cat Cyrus home alone. My sister promised to come in every day to feed him and make sure he was okay but I knew how much he would miss me.

Let me tell you about Cyrus. He's a stunning blue and white Siberian and I inherited him when he was one year old. He used to belong to my aunt, who was a cat breeder, but she died unexpectedly and as I'd bonded well with Cyrus when my aunt was alive I decided to take him on. It was the best decision I ever made. Cyrus was the most affectionate thing I had ever seen. Totally fearless it often felt as if he was protecting me and not the other way around. When we were together at home he would follow me from room to room watching my every move. I loved him to pieces.

I did manage to tear myself away from Cyrus but two weeks into my trip I had this striking dream. Nothing much happened in the dream. In it Cyrus was staring at me intently as he used to whenever we were together, but when I woke up I had this overwhelming sense that he wanted me home. I can't explain why but I just knew I had to get back to the UK, so the following day I made arrangements to fly back a week earlier than planned.

When I got back home Cyrus was delighted to see me but it was clear that my sister had looked after him well. I was a little miffed that I'd cut my vacation short—as I'd been having a fabulous time—but the following day I found out that I had just escaped the tsunami. Cyrus may well have saved my life.

Similar stories of people whose lives quite literally have been saved by cats tend to receive a lot of attention because they are so sensational—and you'll find more dramatic stories like this later in the book—but it is important to point out that such stories are incredibly rare. More common but just as special in their own way are stories about people who haven't necessarily had their lives saved by their pets but still believe that there is a telepathic link between them and their cat. Perhaps some of the following stories sound familiar to you?

I really do think there's a powerful link between Coco and me. I often sense when she wants to come inside. I don't hear her meowing but when I open the door she is there. Or I tell my husband that Coco wants to come in and she is waiting outside. He doesn't even ask me how I know she is outside any more and just opens the door.

Cynthia

Before I got Marmalade I used to need an alarm clock to wake me. I don't need it any more. Fifteen minutes before my alarm clock used to beep I wake up and Marmalade is sitting at the end of my bed staring at me. It's as if he wakes me up with that stare. The incredible thing is that he seems to know when it is the weekend as he always wakes me up an hour later.

Michael

I've got a cat alarm clock. She has been waking me up at the same time for seven years. I don't ever need an alarm call. First she walks across the bed. Then after a few minutes she will start purring really loud. If that doesn't get me to shake a leg she will lie on my face. I can't breathe so I have to get up and have a shower and feed her. She's an incredible clock watcher and is able to figure out daylight saving time for me by waking me up an hour earlier. If I have to get up an hour earlier I always set my alarm clock just in case but I swear she can read it because she wakes me up five or so minutes before it goes off. She behaves more like a watchdog or should I say watchcat.

Paul

My ten-year-old moggie Lucky always knows when I'm pregnant. I'm on my fifth pregnancy now and I got her right after my first child. All through this pregnancy and my others she has been really affectionate, which is different to how she is when I'm not pregnant. She's quite aloof normally and likes to keep herself to herself. She seems to sense when I'm tired or sad. Last year my mother-in-law was diagnosed with cancer and stayed with us for two months before moving to a hospice. Lucky stayed by her side constantly, rarely leaving except to eat and use her litter tray. This was unusual for her as she always sleeps with me, but not then. When the time calls for it she can be so affectionate and I love her dearly for that.

Rachael

My cat always seems to know when I am sad and gives me a lot more attention than normal.

Gina

My cat senses what I'm feeling most of the time. If I'm down with a cold or tummy bug she will hover around me. She is a bit antisocial but when I cry she will put her paws on me and beg for attention. If I'm stressed she will nip at my ankles or do something funny to distract me. I truly believe she knows exactly what is going on with me.

Nina

I believe that cats can sense how you feel too. There was once I was feeling sad and my cat came to me and sat next to me. Usually she only does that when she wants food.

Richard

Last weekend I lost my beloved cat of fifteen years. The pain was pure torture for both myself and my husband. Our children have left home and this cat became like a child to us. Love of cats runs in our family and I was visiting my daughter's house. She has a cat that rarely pays attention to anyone in all the years she has lived there. She comes in to eat and then leaves to wander the streets. Sometimes she will sleep on a settee or my daughter's lap but not often. The most bizarre but amazing thing is that a few days after we lost our cat I visited my daughter and started crying. My daughter's cat jumped up onto my lap—she had never done that to anyone except my daughter before—and started purring and rubbing her head in my hands. My daughter could not believe this sudden change in behaviour. I couldn't either. I just sensed that this cat knew of my loss and was trying to console me.

Belinda

As well as being able to sense when it's time to get up or what their owners are feeling or thinking, cats also seem to be able to sense when their owner is returning home to them.

When I'm not feeling well my cat will always sit with me. You could explain that by biochemical changes in my body that my cat senses but try and explain this one. When I went back home to live with my mother for a few years after my divorce my mother would always have my dinner ready. My job wasn't nine to five so how did she know what time I was going to be back? Because about fifteen to twenty minutes before I got home my cat would sit by the door and start crying. I'm serious. This happened every single time.

Monica

My son's cat always senses when he is going to arrive home and waits at the front door or on the porch to welcome him. My son is a student and even I don't know when he is going to arrive so it is

94

impossible for our cat to know when he is due home. Perhaps the cat's sensitive hearing picks up my son's motorbike before I can. This might explain things if the cat sat down five or ten minutes before he was about to arrive but sometimes the cat waits a good thirty minutes for my son to come home.

Jean

A lot of cat owners have experienced the phenomenon Monica and Jean describe. It's something that is certainly familiar to me. When I lived at home my mum used to say that about five minutes before I walked through the front door my cat Crystal would jump onto the window ledge and start looking out for me. She would do the same even when it was me on the phone. I guess you could explain all this by cats' superior sense of smell or hearing, or an ability to detect subtle atmosphere or mood changes, but I like to think of it as psychic ability. For me there can be no other explanation.

Nurturing your cat's psychic potential

Many cats do appear to have natural psychic powers. For example, people frequently tell me that their cats know when the people they care about are unhappy or not feeling well, even if those people don't show it overtly, or at

95

least not in any way that other humans would recognize. Like humans, some cats are naturally more psychic than others, but if you own a cat and there is a bond of love and trust between you, you can expect your pet at the very least to be sensitive to your moods and feelings because the senses of cats are so keen, especially their intuitive sense.

It goes without saying that an essential requirement for nurturing the psychic potential of your cat is to first of all establish a secure and loving bond with it. If your cat doesn't feel secure and protected by you it's highly unlikely it will be able to tune into your thoughts and feelings. Cats are such independent creatures that they can't be forced to display psychic talents. They must intuitively want to bond with you in this way.

Every cat is different, just as every owner is different, so there are millions of different ways to bond with your cat, and what works for one owner and cat may not necessarily work for another household. Generally though, giving your kitten or cat fresh food, a warm bed, vet care and lots of love and patience tend to work wonders. Many new cat owners make the mistake of thinking that their new pet will instantly want to jump on their lap, but this is not always the case. Bonding with your cat is a delicate and sometimes gradual process and it takes time for them to befriend such a large and often clumsy creature. Taking time to learn about your pet's likes and dislikes, and lots of play and fun time is also a priority. Getting down to the level of your cat by sitting on the floor and letting it come to you can also be a good move. Standing over a cat can make it nervous as you resemble a predator attacking. When petting, rather than lowering your hand from above (too much like a hawk swooping), bring it in from the side or below and slowly work your way to the top of the cat.

Cats love order and routine so try to be as consistent as possible with feed and play times. If your cat will allow, cuddle it a lot too, but if cuddling isn't its thing petting and scratching under the neck or behind the ears surely will be. The time you spend with your cat will help create that loving bond for many years to come. A bond between a cat and an owner can be as intense as that between a child and parent. You love each other and want to be close to one another. You look for comfort in each other. You feel bad when the other feels bad and happy when the other feels happy. No matter what, you are always there for one another.

I truly believe that it is possible for every cat owner to establish a psychic bond with their cat. At the time I didn't realize it, but looking back I can see now that there was a strong psychic connection between me and Crystal, the cat I grew up with. There were many occasions when I believe Crystal tuned into my feelings and thoughts, but one is extremely memorable. My brother had left home for college that morning. I felt intensely lonely and sad. I remember going to my bedroom and hugging my pillow. I looked around for Crystal and felt sad that she wasn't there. I could really have done with her company. Within moments she was there. She jumped onto my bed and laid her warm, purring body on my stomach. It was the best comfort.

Many animal psychics I've talked to over the years have told me that such experiences with cats are not just a coincidence. By using thoughts and feelings they believe that owners can communicate with their cats. They aren't talking about studying your cat's body language or interpreting the sounds it makes. They are talking about transmitting invisible thoughts and feelings to pets on a telepathic wavelength we can all learn to find.

Being so sensitive, cats may just be picking up on subtle aspects of body language in their human companions that indicate sadness or illness, but many animal researchers have not ruled out the possibility of a feline sixth sense. There are scientists—Rupert Sheldrake and J. B. Rhine spring to mind—who believe that a psychic bond exists between pets and their owners, and that cats may indeed be telepathic and clairvoyant.

As far as I'm concerned, it's a bit of a hit-and miss affair whenever I try to communicate silently to Merlin and Max, and I'm not at all confident in my cat communication abilities, but I'm nonetheless convinced that the phenomenon is real.

One exercise I find helpful for nurturing the telepathic bond is to sit quietly with your cat (not at meal times) and to lovingly stroke your pet. Then stop stroking your cat but continue to sit beside it. In your mind but not out loud, tell your cat how much you love and worship it. You may find that your cat continues purring even though you are not stroking or petting, or that the purring becomes even more intense than before. You may need to try this exercise several times to see if you can actually communicate telepathically. It takes time for cats to get used to hearing your thoughts and feelings, so don't give up if you don't see instant results; you need patience. It's also important to stay cool, calm and relaxed, as intuition can never be forced. The best results tend to occur spontaneously.

Even if it takes a while, I still highly recommend the exercise, as both you and your cat will benefit from the stress-reducing close contact you enjoy, which brings us neatly to the subject of the next chapter, the healing power of cats.

4. Healing Cats

There are two means of refuge from the
misery of life—music and cats.

Albert Schweitzer

I don't need any convincing about the
therapeutic power of cats. While writing this
book I found evidence for it all around me
courtesy of the newcomers to my household,
Max and Merlin. Not only have they been
brilliant for my two children—by distracting
them from the lures of TV and PC, and
my husband—who suffers from high blood
pressure and finds their purring incredibly
relaxing—but they have been beneficial for all
of us for the shared time, laughter and
spontaneity they are bringing back into our
lives. I've already mentioned in previous
chapters other healing gifts the kittens have
brought and are bringing me, but one I haven't
mentioned yet but feel is relevant here is the
gift of energy.

I'm not a lazy person but I'm not getting any
younger. Before the kittens arrived getting out
of bed in the morning was starting to get
harder and harder and fatigue was waging war
against me during the day. I don't have that
problem any more. I bounce out of bed early. I

look forward to waking up so I can give the kittens their morning feed and be the one who can see the look on their excited faces as I prepare the food. And, somehow, getting up earlier and at roughly the same time each day has done wonders for my energy levels. I feel ten years younger.

I'm not alone in my belief that cats have healing powers. The letters and emails I've received on this subject certainly merit a chapter of their own. You'll find some of the most memorable stories later in this chapter, but I'd like to kick-start this exploration of healing cats with the story of a celebrity.

Oscar the Death Cat

I've already briefly mentioned the story of Oscar, the cat who lives in an American hospice, in the Introduction, but his story is so remarkable and so relevant to the theme of this chapter that it merits greater discussion and detail here.

In 2005 Oscar was adopted as a kitten by a Rhode Island nursing and rehabilitation centre, where a medical team specializes in late-stage Alzheimer's, Parkinson's and other serious, potentially fatal, illnesses. He never showed much interest in mingling with people, but then nursing staff began to notice that when a person was close to death, in many cases with only hours to live, he would curl up beside them. His predictive abilities have been so accurate that nursing staff now take his presence with a patient as reason enough to notify the family. Just like a doctor Oscar makes his rounds and is serious and dignified in his approach to his work.

After Oscar had accurately predicted his thirteenth case, Dr Jean Teno became convinced of his abilities. According to Teno, the two-year-old cat is more accurate about time of death than the doctors who treat and monitor the patients. When a doctor tells staff to call a patient's family because death is close, if Oscar has not paid the patient a visit the patient typically lives on a few more days. It is not until Oscar makes his final pronouncement with an appearance by the patient's bed that the inevitable happens. If a family member panics and tries to put Oscar outside the patient's bedroom he will pace and meow in front of the closed door, vocalizing his anger. Staff at the medical centre can't explain Oscar's behaviour, but his work is acknowledged and appreciated and a wall plaque commending his 'compassionate hospice care' is being considered.

Oscar's predictive abilities have earned him the nickname the Death Cat, which seems to contradict the theme of this chapter—the healing power of cats—but according to one of the nursing centre's geriatricians, who is also an associate professor of medicine at Brown

University, family members find Oscar's compassion for their dying loved ones incredibly healing and calming. 'He seems to understand when they are going to die,' Dr David Dosa wrote in the *New England Journal of Medicine*.

Not surprisingly Oscar has generated great interest and debate in the medical field among researchers keen to discover the secret of his predictive abilities. Some doctors who have watched him at work have argued that Oscar, like all cats, may have certain sensory perceptions not yet discovered by science that make possible his uncanny forecasts—in other words, a dying person omits a smell or essence that Oscar is attracted to—but to many cat lovers it appears to be much more than that. It's intuition that brings the animal to the dying person, a psychic soul connection.

Not only do the doctors and nurses at the hospice appreciate Oscar's dedication and compassion, they feel his presence has brought healing and comfort to patients and their families, as well as to themselves as they have their own emotions to deal with when a life ends. And for those patients who for some reason or other might be spending their last hours without a loved one present, he or she has the steadfast companionship of a cat who really wears angel wings.

Meet Buckwheat

Oscar's story isn't an isolated one. There are other, less well reported, stories of cats that have gone out of their way to be with a dying person. A matter of weeks after Oscar's story hit the headlines a Seattle nursing home announced that it had its own feline predictor of death.

According to media reports Buckwheat is a ten-year-old tabby donated to the home three years ago by an ailing lady who couldn't look after him any longer. He is a familiar face at the Providence Mount St Vincent nursing home, where staff say that he has been with over thirty patients when they' ve passed. Like Oscar, Buckwheat also seems to have the power to predict when a patient is going to die. And again like Oscar, he does his very best to offer the dying person comfort. The cat will climb on the bed and curl up next to the patient, and will stay through the dying process.

The stories of Oscar and Buckwheat have received media attention, but from speaking to cat owners over the years it is obvious to me that the phenomenon is not uncommon, and there are many other unsung cat healers out there offering end-of-life comfort to those who need it. Take Darcy's moving story, for example.

My mum died last year from liver cancer. She was very strong and did not complain, but it was clear that she was in a lot of pain. I didn't want her to go to a hospice so I cared for her at home. I was warned that in the final few weeks and days it would get very traumatic. My brother and I were worried about how we would comfort her, but drew strength from our prayers.

About a week before Mum died she was on very high doses of morphine but there were moments of lucidity. It was unbearably heartbreaking. One morning I was in the kitchen making what must have been my hundredth cup of coffee—I'd hardly had any sleep in the weeks preceding—and I heard a meowing outside the back door. I opened it and there was this straggly cat standing there. Normally I'd have closed the door quickly to stop the cat coming in, but something—whether it was tiredness or intuition, I don't know— made me hesitate. The cat ran straight upstairs and went into my mum's bedroom, jumped on her bed and curled into a ball beside her.

My mum was sleeping peacefully, so I tiptoed to the bed and tried to take the cat away but she just jumped over my mum to the other side of the bed. The movement must have woken my mum as she opened her eyes. When she saw the cat she smiled and shook her head at me as if to say leave things be, so I retreated and left the two of them sleeping together.

For the next two days this cat never left my mum's side except for meal times—we fed him white fish—and to go to the toilet outside. My mum had been very unsettled and uncomfortable, but now with the cat curled up beside her she seemed much more peaceful.

When Mum died we decided to keep the cat because he found a new job—for want of a better word—and that job was to comfort Dad. Dad missed my mum terribly when she was gone, and the cat seemed to sense that and was his constant companion.

Allen's mother also received the comfort and love of a cat in her final moments.

Casey, my feisty tabby cat, who normally likes to keep himself to himself, climbed into Mum's bed and lay down on her stomach about two hours before she died. My sister lifted him off but he just climbed back on again. Casey had never been very affectionate with anyone, especially my mother, who preferred dogs, so this did surprise me. I found his behaviour impossible to understand until I did some reading and found out about Oscar.

Stories like those of Darcy and Allen reinforce my belief that there is an unexplained and possibly mystic connection between animals and humans and that this connection manifests itself very strongly when we are at our most vulnerable and needy. There is perhaps no time in our lives when we are more vulnerable and needy than when death is close.

Stay with me

I have known cats to behave in this way when there is a death in the family. When my mother was diagnosed with cancer she owned a cat called Sam. She got Sam a year or two after I left home so I didn't get a chance to bond with him, as I had done with Crystal. It would have been hard to bond with him anyway as he was an aloof British blue who really didn't like a lot of fuss made over him. The only person he showed affection to was my mum, but he never slept on her bed or settled on her lap for more than a few moments. I know my mum would have dearly liked to feel closer to Sam, but she didn't try to force things and accepted him for the independent and self-assured cat he was.

A few weeks before my mum died Sam started to spend most of the day and night

107

lying next to her on the bed. Immediately after Mum had been diagnosed with cancer I talked to her about going into a hospice because the doctor told me that it was only a matter of time before she needed care 24/7. A hospice seemed the best solution but she refused to leave home. She wanted to die on her own terms and I respected her wishes. It did leave me in a horrible dilemma though. I was in my mid-twenties and trying to establish a career for myself. I could resign but with the doctor saying she could live anywhere between one and five years there was no guarantee of my employability at the end. I was torn between career worries about getting into debt and love for my mother, and I don't think I coped very well.

I now realize that millions of people face a similar dilemma when loved ones get sick or need round-the-clock care, but back then I felt so alone. Mum and Dad lived separate lives and my brother was abroad so I was the only one. I had no one to turn to so I decided to compromise. I would work a four-day week, take care of my mum at the weekends and organize a home help for the other three days. I figured this arrangement would work in the short term and then I would have a rethink if her condition deteriorated. I didn't really think that would happen though. I was convinced Mum would get better.

Watching someone you love fade away is an

unbearably painful experience. I dealt with it by refusing to accept what was happening. All my life my mum had been a tower of strength; I had no doubt in my mind that she would pull through. I was young and naïve and could not accept that she was going to die. But die she did at 2.11 on a cold and dark Tuesday afternoon in November.

At her last home check-up the doctor had told me she was doing as well as could be expected and was not close to the point of death so I had no reason to believe it would be the last time I spoke to her when I said goodbye before heading off to work in the morning. The home help was due to visit in a few hours and Sam was settled in his usual position close by her side.

Although Mum looked weak, jaundiced and fretful as I left her room, she was stroking Sam from time to time and I told myself this was a very positive sign. Sam had been a constant presence in her bedroom for the last two weeks and I knew how much Mum had wanted to bond with him so this made me smile inside. When the phone call came through to me at work that afternoon from the home help that she had died it was like a hammer blow to my heart. It took weeks for the news to sink in, and when I finally accepted the reality of it, I blamed myself. I hated myself for not staying with my mum that morning. I should have been there. Then at least she would have died with her daughter by her side and not a stranger. I longed to turn back time—to reverse my decision to go to work that morning.

In the months and years that followed I never stopped beating myself up for not being with my mother when she died. I hated myself for putting myself first. Guilt and sadness about my mum's lonely death were never far away and somehow always seemed to surface whenever I felt close to happiness. It wasn't until three years later that the journey towards healing and self-forgiveness began when a letter arrived from a lady called Sheila.

The letter was very long, so for the sake of brevity I will paraphrase it here. Basically Sheila told me that she had adopted Sam from the RSPCA two years before and she wanted to thank me for handing him in. She told me that when she was seriously ill with glandular fever Sam, who normally stayed outside during the day, had changed his routine and snuggled up to her on the sofa. Sam's comfort and warmth had made all the difference to her recovery. She told me that Sam had done the same when her husband went down with a bout of flu. They both dearly loved Sam and wanted me to know what a special cat he was.

When I read the letter it felt like a light bulb had switched on in my heart. I still wished that I'd been there for her, but Mum hadn't been alone and without love and warmth when she died. Sam had been there all the time easing her transition from this world into the next. It felt like a weight had dropped off my shoulders.

After Mum's death I had no option but to take Sam to the RSPCA. I didn't have the money or the living space to accommodate a cat. It was a tough decision to make but at the time it was the right one. I was struck down with grief and could barely look after myself, let alone a cat. I wrote back to Sheila to thank her for letting me know and to tell her more about the circumstances leading up to Sam going to the RSPCA.

It may have taken me several years to fully comprehend just how much Sam must have been a comfort to my mum when she died, but I never stop thanking him in my heart for what he did. I now realize that by helping both the dying and their loved ones through the transition known as death, ordinary cats like Sam—just like their famous counterparts—show us the meaning of love as well as how to love. Even unconscious I believe that the dying are still capable of sensing the vibration of love, and surely it was love and comfort that Sam was offering my mother, unconditional love that makes no demands.

We all long for that kind of love, but what we don't realize is that it is available right now if we can open our hearts to the animal teachers willing to show the dying the way to love.

Being a cat person myself I love the idea of a cat being with me at the end of my life. And it's not just the dying who are comforted by the presence of a cat, but also loved ones coping with the confusion, emptiness, guilt and grief. I've heard many stories about cats showing empathy towards people suffering bereavement. I've chosen to include Liz's story here, sent to me via email, because I think it shows in a beautiful but simple way that if there is any force strong enough to counteract the grief of bereavement it's love. And love, and lots of it, is exactly what cats can and do offer their owners.

IT TAKES THREE

When Dad died Mum was raw with grief. I didn't want to leave her alone so I made her stay with us. I was worried about her. She'd been married to Dad for nearly fifty years and they had only had a few nights apart in all that time. I've got three cats and it was like they had an arrangement between them, because every night one or two of them would be sleeping on the bed with her. We don't normally allow our cats to do this but we could see the comfort it was giving her so we allowed it. She stayed for three months with us and then much to our surprise told us she was fine to move back to her house, as long as she could take the cats with her. If the kids had still been at home this would not have worked as they would never have let us, but with my youngest now at college I let them go. I miss them greatly but they belong with Mum now, not with us.

Laura has a similar tale to share.

SUCH A BLESSING

When my wife passed away suddenly last year a lot of my friends suggested I get a pet to keep me company. We never had children or pets so it was a first for me. I thought it was worth a try so I went to a cattery and my life changed the moment I saw Samson. He's nearly two years old now and I renamed him Locket because the first thing he played with when we got home was the locket with my picture in that my wife used to wear every day. He's a calico or black-and-red-coloured British short hair with copper-coloured eyes.

I injured my back a few months after I'd got him and had to go and stay with my brother and his wife for nearly ten days. I missed Locket very much and he now is constantly by my side. He sleeps on my bed—takes up most of it, in fact—and wakes me up every morning. He loves to be hugged and to play. He's a real blessing and my best friend.

Cats can teach us a lot about coping with death and coping with the reality of dying—and we'll return to this important theme in later chapters—but, as mentioned previously, it's not just when death is close that cats offer their unique brand of warmth and comfort. I've lost count of the many stories I've heard and read about cats who watch over their owners whenever they feel sick or sad.

Cat therapy

The value of cats as therapeutic animals is gradually being recognized not just by their owners but by doctors, therapists, convalescent homes and other healing institutions. It's incredible to see patients' eyes light up whenever a cat is brought in, and even more fortunate are those patients in nursing homes with a cat in residence. I know myself how relaxing and wonderful it can be to pet a cat at the end—or beginning—of a busy day when you're feeling stressed or low. I can feel my muscles and my shoulders relax, and as stress flows out of my body, pleasure floods in. In an instant worries are forgotten and the pressures and strains of daily life disappear.

Sometimes it's virtually impossible to drag yourself away from the relaxing spell of a cat. While working on this book I experienced the true power of that spell. I'd been playing with and cuddling Merlin, and just before he fell asleep he had purred loudly and rolled onto his back. He was curling his chin up in that gorgeous way cats do and it was so cute. Tiptoeing away to my desk wasn't an option because Merlin had fallen asleep on my skirt. I was wearing a really long floaty garment and hadn't noticed that he was lying on part of it. The moment was so magical that I didn't want to spoil it, so I just sat there gazing at him for a good half an hour while he napped. The phone rang while I sat there and I heard the caller leave a message that I'd been offered a potentially lucrative book deal. In the past before cats—bc as we call it now—I'd have jumped to the phone in excitement, but now with Merlin asleep on my skirt everything would have to wait. (Ridiculous, I know. My husband tells me I'm well on the way to becoming a crazy cat lady. I remind him that over a third of the stories I've collected have been from men, and more often than not they are just as passionate, if not more so, in their praise of cats.)

To return to the theme: a while back I read about a programme in Newcastle where elderly people in a care home were given a pet for a month. They were asked to rate their quality of life before and after, and all rated it higher after a month with pets. Although dogs are traditionally recruited as therapy animals,

I'm not surprised that cats are being used more and more. Dogs are great but cats have the huge advantage of being able to purr. Recent studies have validated what many cat lovers already instinctively know—that being around a contented, purring cat can drop a human's high blood pressure to within normal range, decrease stress, conquer feelings of loneliness and even bolster self-confidence.

Linda certainly knows the value of spending time with her cat.

ALWAYS MAKES ME FEEL HAPPY

Whenever I'm in need of a boost my cat Rusty is there for me. He snuggles up to me and is so loving, sometimes more than any man or person could be. He loves me unconditionally and he has helped me get through so many times of crisis. He always makes me feel happy and better somehow.

I think many cat owners would agree that somehow, even when things aren't going well in their daily lives, their cats always make them feel better. I love this little story sent to me via email by Sally a few years back. Again I think so many cat owners will relate to it.

Pansy, my cat, has this brilliant personality. She always makes me happy when I'm sad or angry. Even if my boyfriend and I fight and we see Pansy look at us with those big eyes or do something else cute we can't help but laugh and talk about how cute she is. I'm not joking. It's tough to fight when she is around and she has really healed my home life. My boyfriend proposed last month. I'm not sure though if it's me or Pansy that he wants ? .

Few cat owners would deny that cats have this ability to raise our spirits, but as Cara's extraordinary story shows their healing power can sometimes extend far beyond that.

THIS IS FOR LIFE

I suffer from autism, not a severe form of autism when I can't communicate with others or show empathy but a milder form (I think doctors call it high functioning), when it doesn't take much for me to snap and go into meltdown. You could say I lack patience. But since owning cats from the age of twenty-five—I'm nearly forty now— I have become more patient and understanding not just to animals but to people. Currently I own two cats, a boy and a girl called Muffin and Pumpkin, and they mean the world to me. Over the years that I've owned cats I have had fewer and fewer breakdowns, and if things aren't going well I look to my cats for the calm I am lacking

117

inside. I know I will always live with cats. Life would not taste good without them.

People with milder forms of autism need a living being to connect with who seems to understand them, and it appears from stories like Cara's that cats can provide that kind of mentoring, because they are patient. Trudie certainly believes that a cat is helping to bring her autistic son out of the darkness and into the light.

OUT OF THE DARKNESS

My seven-year-old son suffers from Asperger's syndrome. Until we brought Tyler, a moggie with a touch of Bombay about him, into the home he found it hard to understand that other people have feelings, and he struggled with communication, having a limited vocabulary.

When my best friend had a litter of kittens to give away, at first I was unsure because my son had terrorized my brother's cat by chasing him and pulling his tail, but I was at my wits' end and thought I would give it a try. So we brought the cat home and named him Tyler, and it was like a light switch turned on in my son. He talked to the cat all day long.

Tyler bonded with my son from the very

first day and will chirp and purr and cuddle with him all the time. He will also put up with being carried everywhere and sleeps with my son, which must be an ordeal as my son also suffers from restless legs syndrome. Tyler will just sit and listen to my son when he talks and talks, and I sometimes think only Tyler can really understand what my son is saying. Thanks to Tyler, my son now has a friend, someone to talk to and play with and cuddle, but best of all it is thanks to Tyler that my son is learning to show empathy and respect to someone else. We have had Tyler nearly a year now and he's so much more than a cat to us. He's a member of our family. He's brought our son out of the darkness.

Here's another astonishing cat healing story, sent to me by Monica.

ABOUT CHARLIE

I work as a care assistant in a nursing home for the elderly; have done for more years than I care to remember now. It's heartbreaking to see so many old people spend their final years in isolation. I do my best but I can't be a friend to all of them, and some of them have turned so inwards that they don't even want to talk to me. I truly believe that the most serious disease for old people is not cancer or dementia but loneliness, and I also believe that pets, especially cats, can be part of the solution.

Five years ago I met this lady called Rose. She didn't seem to have anyone, no family and no friends. She had little interest in living. When I tried to interact with her or even feed and wash her she would say over and over again, 'Leave me be, leave me be.' She would spend her days and nights curled up in a foetal position. She had terrible bed sores and would scratch her legs until they bled.

Then this beautiful cat—I think he was Persian, but I'm no cat expert so can't be sure—called Charlie was brought into the home. All the residents fussed over him constantly and he ended up seeking refuge in Rose's bedroom because it was always so quiet with no visitors. Charlie slept on the floor of Rose's room for a few nights and then he started to jump onto her bed. When he was on her bed, whenever Rose tried to curl up her legs he would lie on her stomach, so she was forced to stretch out, and when she tried to scratch her legs he would nibble at her hands so she got distracted.

Within two months Rose was sitting up in bed and had stopped scratching herself. The most incredible thing about all this is that she loved the cat so much that she asked staff if she could take care of him and if he could become her cat. There was heated debate about this at the time as lots of residents were fond of him, but he had so clearly become Rose's cat that it was decided that Charlie should become known as her cat. When Rose was told of the decision she started inviting other residents to come and visit her in her room to play with Charlie, and there was a constant stream of visitors from then onwards.

The therapeutic value of cats for the elderly and infirm is undeniable, and reports of cats like Caiu, an affable five-year-old Maine Coon half-orange tabby who lives in the Nazareth Classic Care Community in Menlo Park in California, are becoming more and more common. Twice a month Caiu makes his rounds of the long-term care facility for Alzheimer's and dementia patients, bringing a smile to their faces and sometimes helping them to reconnect with the present.

The value of cats as companions and healers is being recognized not just in the USA but all over the world. In the UK hundreds of cats trained by pet therapy organizations silently and lovingly work their unique brand of healing magic every day. And it's not just the elderly or those in hospitals and nursing homes who report beneficial effects during times of illness. The theme running through the following stories, beginning with this delightful one sent into me by Kim, is the loving presence of a cat sensing its owner's feelings and aiding their recovery.

MY NURSE CATS

My cats always know when I'm not well. If I'm ill Oscar will smell my face and then stretch himself out on my stomach. When my dad died last year Oscar knew that things weren't right with me and followed me everywhere. Oscar keeps my blood pressure down—of that I am sure. I also suffer from migraines. I'll lie down with a cold flannel on my head and Oscar will climb onto my head. If I am sitting, Oscar will jump on my lap and try to work his way up to my shoulders and balance there. He never manages it and his efforts always make me laugh, which I guess is healing in itself when you're in so much pain.

And my other cat, Fudge, is getting so good at predicting when I'm going to get an attack. Fudge will walk along the back of the sofa and then try to climb on my head. An hour or so later I come down with a migraine. Fudge has gotten so good at predicting this that I take my medication right away. I have no idea how she knows, but I sure am glad she helps me out like this as anyone who has ever had a migraine will tell you what a curse they are.

Kim believes that her cats just know when something isn't right with her, and every day she is grateful for their watchfulness. Zack is also intensely grateful for the watchfulness and healing love that his cat Grace gives to him.

GOOD GRACE

When I was seventeen I had a fall when I was out skateboarding and injured my head seriously. I was examined but I looked normal and doctors couldn't find anything wrong with me. They did warn me of the risk of seizures though. After my accident my cat Grace started to behave strangely. Some days she would weave in and out of my feet, making me trip up or forcing me to sit down. She would also meow really loudly, but when I offered her food she would turn it down. Anyway for no apparent reason she would do everything in her power to stop me leaving the house or sometimes my bedroom. The first time she did this I had a seizure, but fortunately I was at home so my mum could take care of me. Then a few weeks later the same thing happened. Grace wouldn't let me leave my bedroom and ran backwards and forwards in front of me and made me lie down on my bed. I had a seizure. It's happened so many times now that when Grace does actually let me out of her sight Mum and my friends and even my doctor laugh and say, 'There but for the grace of his cat, he goes.'

Zack's story is incredible, but one thing I have learned from hearing and reading so many cat healing stories over the years is that cats are full of wonderful surprises. Just when you think you've heard the most remarkable story, you stumble across another one which is just as astonishing, and then another and another.

Here's Shirley's compelling story.

SPOOK

I can't imagine living without a cat. There have always been cats in my life from as early as I remember. I grew up with them. I was nineteen when I got Spook. I was leaving home for the first time into my own little flat and she was a gift from Mum and Dad to keep me company. I called her Spook because apart from tiny dashes of black on the right side of her face she was completely white and looked like a ghost. She was with me when I left home, got my first job, and she was with me through several relationships, redundancy, marriage and pregnancy. She was with me

124

when I became a single mum to my only daughter, Victoria.

I didn't have an easy pregnancy, I was violently sick for most of it. The birth was tough too and in the weeks and months after I suffered from post-natal depression and my partner left me. We tried to salvage things for Victoria's sake but there was no going back when I found out he was having an affair with my best friend. My heart was broken in two places by the people I had loved and trusted the most. My partner moved out leaving me and Victoria alone.

So there I was, an inexperienced mum with a six-month-old baby to care for alone. I would cry for days, weeks on end. Victoria was a fussy baby and would only sleep for a few hours at a time. When she was awake the only thing that would stop her screaming was being walked around and gently bounced. If I tried to do anything else when holding her, like listening to the radio or reading a magazine, she would scream. It was an ordeal. She demanded every bit of my attention, and I have to admit that I started to resent her. I wasn't sure whether I loved her. I even considered adoption, I was feeling that low.

When I first brought Victoria home, Spook just seemed to vanish, only appearing for meal times. She must have found the sound of Victoria crying very unsettling. I do remember thinking, that makes two of us. When my partner left and the rowing stopped, Spook started to become less wary. She would even venture into a room when we were in it and sit staring at us. I found her presence comforting. Whenever Victoria was asleep she would curl up beside me, purring loudly.

There is one incident I remember clearly. I'd spent ages rocking Victoria asleep and had managed to gently place her in the nursery. As I tiptoed out in the semi-darkness I accidentally stepped on a musical toy and its loud and merry chimes immediately set Victoria off crying. I kicked the toy as it had been a gift from her dad and at that moment my blood was boiling with anger. It felt like the last straw, and instead of attending to Victoria I just slumped down on the floor and put my hands over my ears to block out the crying. I cried and cried.

A moment or so later I felt a wet nose and whiskers brush my hands. It was Spook. I had never been so glad to see her at that moment. She jumped onto my stomach and looked in the direction of Victoria crying as if to tell me to settle her down. Feeling calmer and a little stronger I got up and lifted Victoria gently out of her cot. I rocked her and within ten minutes she was asleep.

Looking back I now realize how tough it must have been for Spook to come up to me like that. She had always hated screaming and crying, but there she was with me in the nursery standing by and watching while the two of us were crying. After that special moment she lost her fear of Victoria and was always by my side whether she was crying or sleeping. When Victoria did cry I knew that Spook would have dearly loved to disappear and find a place of refuge, but her constant companionship, love and courage helped me discover a strength and calmness within myself that I didn't know I had.

Victoria is close to two years old now. Spook still hovers around me but she is less watchful than a year or so ago because I think she knows that I can cope now and am actually starting to enjoy being a mum. She will even let Victoria stroke her. I know she can't stand it when Victoria tries to pick her up, but she takes it all in good humour and once again she is teaching me volumes about love and understanding.

Arseiny also believes that his cat helps him cope with periods of depression.

I suffer from panic attacks and episodes of depression. I've been on anti-depressants for many years and some days it is difficult to leave my house. When my girlfriend left me two years ago I decided to adopt a kitten. I had had a cat when I was a child and knew what great companions they could be. I didn't want to be alone. So Henry became a part of my life in early 2007. Instantly I felt that I had a purpose. I took care of him and then a few months later decided he needed company—just like I did—and so I adopted another kitten. The RSPCA told me that it might not work out as Henry had established himself as my cat but it did. My second cat, Rusty, is a laid-back character, and within days the two of them were rushing around my house getting into all sorts of scraps. They were hilarious. I don't think I have laughed so much in years.

Henry and Rusty are such a great distraction. I don't have time any more to be depressed, and whenever black feelings hit me I just need to spend some time with them. I feel I can handle my life a little better now and I don't get any panic attacks any more. I'm hopelessly addicted to them, in fact, and coming home to my two cats is the best part of my day. I feel I can tell them all my worries. I don't know why people say they are solitary and aloof creatures. They are the most loving therapists and my best friends.

Lucy shared a similar experience with me. Here's her story.

THE BEST THERAPIST MONEY CAN BUY

My chocolate-brown and white cat, Buttons, is the best therapist money can buy. I adopted her when my friend left to live in the States. Originally I was only going to keep her for a few months and then rehome her with someone else, but I got so attached to her that I thought I would rather live on the streets than give her up. I suffer from bipolar disorder, and I feel that it is only Buttons who takes me for what I am. When I get very low it is Buttons that saves me and I will always be so grateful. She just knows when I am not feeling good. She will climb on my shoulder and nip at my neck and it never fails to make me smile, even if I don't feel that I want to.

The theme of cats being great therapists is one that Veronica wrote to tell me she wholeheartedly agrees with.

Ten years ago I had a nervous breakdown. I was out of work for a year. I attended weekly sessions with a therapist but there were things about my life that I found extremely difficult to talk to my therapist about. Then one day the therapist's cat was asleep on the floor when I came in. The therapist asked me if I was okay with this or if I wanted the cat to be put outside. The cat looked blissfully happy. I didn't want it moved so we began our session. About five minutes into the session the cat looks at me and rolls halfway onto its back with its paws in the air, purring. I remember thinking what an open, trusting position that was to take, and with my attention divided between the cat and the therapist without even realizing it I made more progress in that session than I had done since I started.

I have no doubt that this cat was very helpful to my eventual recovery. He joined us for most of my remaining sessions. He had this thing about rubber bands and would suddenly pounce on my therapist's desk if he saw one. I have my own cat now. He's called Pickles and his presence is just as beneficial to me because I feel I can tell him anything and that he is listening to me with his heart. Pickles was a stray nobody wanted, so I gave him a home. Like me he had a tough time but he has pulled through and has now grown into a magnificent tom currently playing with my laptop as I try to type this!!!

Purr power

When I suffered a miscarriage last year I was devastated. There's not much other people can say or do to make you feel better. I was in mourning but my Abyssinian cat Sugar offered me more comfort and reassurance than any human. Whenever I cried she purred her loudest and wouldn't leave me alone. She definitely sensed my emotions and helped me recover. She couldn't talk to me but she communicated such deep love and empathy to me, when I needed it the most. She really helped me out.

Nadia

I have nerve disease in my right leg and the pain is at its worst at night. Painkillers aren't as effective as my cat Pepper. He comes and sits on my leg and plays the piano, as I like to call it, with his paws. He purrs all the time and gives me such warmth and comfort. The pain usually eases and sometimes disappears, and I can get a good night's sleep.

Michael

It's common knowledge among cat lovers that cats have the ability to boost our mood and offer comfort when we are unwell. How many times has your cat curled up beside you and started purring and instantly stress washes away? Talk to any cat lover and it really does appear that cats can sense our pain, both emotional and physical, and help relieve it. Even more surprising is that there is now scientific evidence to prove that cat lovers aren't imagining all this: a cat's purr really does have the power to help us heal.

Vets will tell you how quickly the bones of cats mend compared to dogs, and some cat researchers believe that a cat's purr could be the healing mechanism to explain this. This is because documentation suggests that frequencies between 25 and 50 hertz are best for relieving pain and promoting bone growth, muscle repair and fracture healing. A cat's purr, regardless of size and breed, is within this frequency range. To prove the theory of the healing power of purring, researchers have used sensitive monitors on domestic cats. The cats were not harmed in any way and during the experiment were encouraged to purr by stroking and petting. The study showed that cats produce frequencies when they purr that have been shown to improve healing time, and this could go some way towards explaining many stories of cat therapy. It looks like nature has blessed cats with a self-healing ability in their purr, and so when people say their cats make them feel better, it's very possible that this is because purring acts as a low-vibration therapy that eases pain and strengthens our bodies. Other studies have confirmed that stroking a cat can lower blood pressure and boost mood. Who knows? Perhaps one day doctors may tell their patients, 'Take one cat, and come back and see me next week.'

The scientific explanation of purring is certainly fascinating but it doesn't explain how cats often just seem to know when their owners are feeling under the weather and in need of some purr therapy. For many people it's not just a cat's purr but its intuitive ability to sense when its owner is in need of comfort that is the true miracle. Their sixth sense that things aren't well with its owner and that some love and comfort is needed can be just as therapeutic as the purr itself.

Sometimes a cat will even sense that someone is in need of comfort and love before they realize it themself. I've found this happen many times myself. I'll get carried away with a project I'm working on and then suddenly Max and Merlin will jump onto my desk and lie down on my books as if to say enough is enough, time for bed or a snack. Usually when

I look at my watch I realize that I've been bashing away at the keyboard for hours without stopping, and for my health and wellbeing I should take a break.

So the next time your cat is eager to sit with you or nap on your work let your pet work its curative magic. Especially on those days when you aren't feeling your best snuggle down into the warmth of your sofa or bed with them. Not only is this a great way to de-stress and relax, but as we've seen there are scientifically proven therapeutic benefits for both your body and your mind as well.

Take time out to listen to a cat purr—it truly is gorgeous and one of nature's most healing sounds.

5. Heroes with Whiskers and Fur

The cat could very well be man's best friend but would never stoop to admitting it.

Doug Larson

A cat sensing and healing its owner's pain, and in some cases predicting it before it happens, is remarkable enough, but in this chapter we shall look at cats who have gone way beyond the call of duty and actually saved the lives of their owners.

You may have read stories in the newspapers or seen reports on television about dogs that do heroic deeds. Reports of cats saving lives and warning their owners of danger are less well circulated—perhaps because their owners aren't interested in the publicity—but I have heard and read many stories over the years from people who believe their courageous cats are heroes. There are stories of cats waking people to warn them of fires or natural disasters, cats who put themselves in harm's way to save their owners and cats using their psychic powers to alert their owners to potential danger.

Carol's story about her cat is heart-warming, and a great way to start this chapter.

CASPAR

I've shared my life with Caspar for seven years now. I know everyone thinks their cat is the most beautiful cat in the world but everyone who sees him loves him. He's a cream tabby and white Maine Coon and so gentle and loyal. He never leaves my side and follows me everywhere. One day about two years ago now he followed me into the kitchen but when I got there I felt my head spinning. I knew something wasn't right so I turned around to grab my phone in the living room but I don't think I got very far. I must have fainted and collapsed.

My memory isn't very clear but I do recall drifting in and out of consciousness. Every time I opened my eyes Caspar was there licking my cheeks and meowing loudly. It helped me stay conscious long enough to crawl into the living room and grab my mobile to call for help. I honestly think that if Caspar hadn't been there I would not be writing this today. He never left my side until the ambulance people arrived.

I stayed in hospital for two days while doctors ran tests. I suffer from high blood pressure and was diagnosed with an irregular heartbeat. I'm now on medication to treat it but I do sometimes still feel extremely tired. Caspar keeps a close eye on me though, and every so often when I lie down to rest he will jump up beside me on the bed and headbutt me to check I'm okay.

Caspar takes such good care of me and I love him deeply. He is very protective and loving and everyone falls under his spell when they meet him. I wanted to share my story with you because I believe it shows that cats sense and understand so much more than we think they do. I believe every cat, given love and the opportunity to bond with an owner, can become like my Caspar—an angel.

This next story came from Pam. It's similar to the one above, but like every cat story I've heard or read it's also completely unique.

SUPER CAT

I was up very late one night. I'd stayed up to watch the movie *The Sixth Sense*. My husband Ron had gone to bed an hour ago. I'd never seen the movie before and found it absorbing but absolutely terrifying. I was so grateful for the company of Frankie, my gorgeous tabby. It was gone two o' clock in the morning when the film finished and I scolded myself for staying up so late. When you're in your seventies like me it's best to get your head down early and rise early. As I headed upstairs Frankie brushed past me. It freaked me out a bit and I could feel my heart beating very fast. I went into the bathroom to brush my teeth and then it is all a total blank for me.

I've got to go with my husband Ron's version of events now as I was out cold. According to Ron, Frankie ran into his bedroom and jumped onto his bed and started to meow very loudly. Ron's a very deep sleeper and it takes a lot to wake him, so Frankie—no spring chicken herself at the age of sixteen—must have had to work very hard. Eventually Ron got out of bed and followed Frankie into the bathroom, where he found me in a messy heap on the floor. He called an ambulance right away.

Later I found out that I'd had a mild stroke. It was a real wake-up call not to take my health and my life for granted. I'm so grateful to Frankie for saving my life. My heart may be slowing down but it's so comforting knowing that she was there to keep it warm.

Mona Bastian contacted me from the USA to tell me the story of her cat.

LUCKY

I called my cat Lucky because she was lucky to be alive. She was the runt of a litter of cats and because she wasn't the best-looking cat she was also the last one to find a home. I got the feeling when I came to visit her at the age of sixteen weeks that lots of people had seen her and that if I hadn't taken her the owner was going to have her put down. She was a mess of black and white spots and stripes and straggly long hair, and it was impossible to call her cute, but for me there was something endearing about her. What can I say? Our eyes met and I knew I was going to take her home. What I didn't realize at the time was that I was the lucky one.

138

For fourteen years Lucky shared my life. She was loving and affectionate to me but disappeared when other people were around. I think she liked it best when it was just the two of us. One night she started to act very strange. I heard her meowing outside my back door. I opened the door to let her in but she wouldn't come inside. Stepping outside to investigate I saw her race down my yard and sit in front of the gate as if she wanted to get out. This was unusual because all these years Lucky had always been perfectly content to remain in my backyard—it's very spacious. Dismissing it as just one of those things I went back inside but moments after I'd closed the door Lucky was at it again—meowing even louder than before. Again when I opened the door she raced down and started scratching at the back gate.

This intrigued me, so I grabbed my coat and some shoes and went outside to investigate. When I got to the back gate I heard a faint moaning sound. I was frightened now so I tried to grab Lucky and go back inside. She slipped through my fingers as I reached down and ran back towards the gate. The moaning sound got louder so I called 911. I wasn't going to take any chances.

Fortunately I didn't have to wait too long for her. There were officers in my area and they were ringing at my doorbell ten or so minutes later. When they opened my back gate and shone their torches up the street they found a woman lying on the ground. She had a terrible gash on her head and there was blood everywhere. An ambulance took her to hospital and later I discovered that she had been attacked several hours earlier as she walked home. I was also told that if she had lain there for any longer she may not have survived. Lucky had saved her life.

The story of Lucky doesn't end there. Turns out this woman was very wealthy and she insisted that I be rewarded. I refused at first and told her it wasn't me but my cat, but she said the kindest thing to me in a letter when she enclosed a very generous cheque. She said that she was a cat lover herself and believed that the love and care I had given Lucky had helped him become such a remarkable and compassionate cat. I donated half the money to a cat shelter in my area and used the other half to treat myself and Lucky to a comfortable new settee—she's busy scratching it as I write this now.

This reminds me of another remarkable story I read online a few years ago in June 2007. The story is from Rotorua, New Zealand and appeared in the *Herald News*.

Sylvester the cat, a ginger-cross Persian adopted by ninety-year-old owner Patricia Kerr five years ago, saved the life of his owner when she was found stuck in a cold bath in her home. The cat sensing something was wrong turned up at a neighbour's door and started to make a lot of noise. The neighbours—Shirley and Monte Mason—knew Sylvester to be an antisocial cat so they took it as a sign that Mrs Kerr might be in trouble.

Mrs Mason phoned Mrs Kerr, her neighbour for twenty years, and was reassured that she was okay when she heard that the phone was engaged. She and her husband then went out for a few hours. When they returned they saw that Mrs Kerr had not left her rubbish bag out as normal for Mr Mason to put on the street. Mrs Mason phoned again and again and each time the phone was engaged. Starting to get very worried they eventually went next door and walked around the house peering in at the windows and calling out to their neighbour. When Mrs Kerr did not respond they called the police, who broke into the house and found Mrs Kerr stuck in her bath.

It was not known how long Mrs Kerr had

been in the bath but the water was very cold and she had gone hypothermic. Mrs Kerr was taken to hospital to recover, and according to media reports if she had not been found she could very easily have died. According to the Masons if it had not been for Sylvester alerting them to the fact that something was wrong they may well not have worried about the missing rubbish bag and Mrs Kerr might have been found dead, rather than alive.

Also on the Internet (*Insurance Journal, Midwest News*) is the story of Tommy, a cat from Columbus, Ohio whose breathtaking cleverness saved his owner's life.

HE'S MY HERO

Police simply can't find any other way to explain it but when an officer entered an apartment in early January 2006 in response to a 911 call there was an orange and tan striped cat lying beside a telephone on the living-room floor. The owner of the cat, Gary Rosheisen, was found on the ground having fallen out of his wheelchair.

According to Rosheisen, his cat, Tommy, hit the correct buttons to call 911. Officer Patrick Daugherty, who attended the scene, admits that 'it sounds kind of weird' but isn't sure how else to explain it.

Rosheisen said he couldn't get up from the floor because of the pain he suffers from osteoporosis and ministrokes that alter his sense of balance. He also wasn't wearing his medical alert necklace and couldn't reach a cord above his bed to alert paramedics that he was in trouble and needed help. Rosheisen got Tommy three years ago to help him relax and to help lower his blood pressure. He tried to train him to call 911 but he wasn't sure if the training had worked. Rosheisen's living-room phone is always on the floor and there are twelve small buttons—including a speed dial for 911 right above the button for the speaker phone.

Officer Daugherty said that police received a 911 call from Rosheisen's apartment but when they answered there was no reply. Police called back to see if everything was okay but when no one answered they decided to visit the apartment. This is when Daugherty found Tommy sitting beside the phone and Rosheisen on the floor.

'He's my hero,' says Rosheisen.

A week before this book was due to be delivered I was fortunate enough to be sent this deeply personal story from a lady I'll call Sarah. Her story only deepens the mystery of cats and is so inspiring I had to find a way to include it in this chapter.

SAPPHIRE

Depression has always hounded me like a black dog. Each time I fall into the darkness I wonder if the light will ever shine again. My cat Sapphire dreads the darkness that falls on me as much as I do because she knows that when I'm low and crying I'm pretty useless. I won't play with her, change her litter tray or give her tasty treats to eat like I do when I'm feeling better. She'll try all sorts of things to get my attention. If I'm crying on the bed she will jump on it and then start purring so loud her whole body shakes.

Her antics do often help me but two months ago even Sapphire wasn't enough. My husband filed for divorce and said he was going to take the kids. I didn't have any fight left in me and I figured everyone would be better off without me. I just wanted to end it. I got drunk and started grabbing pills from the cabinet and throwing them on the floor. I didn't even know what they were—some of them had been hanging around in my bathroom for years. There I was sitting on the floor surrounded by pills, trying to kill myself, when my cat saved my life. Sapphire, who doesn't like to be held and never sits on my lap, jumped onto my lap and started to purr. It wasn't her normal loud purr but a gentle calming purr. She talked to me like this for a good hour and it stopped me moving about and reaching for any more pills. I sobbed all my pain and heartache to poor Sapphire and she just sat on my lap listening.

After that point, although the darkness still comes back to haunt me from time to time, thanks to Sapphire I've not sunk as low again. Sometimes I think Sapphire can read my mind. Whenever I start thinking that I'm useless and there's no point getting on with my day she will meow and somehow manage to get me up and doing. She'll demand food or bully me for attention and then it will hit me. Sapphire needs me. As depressed as I may feel I need to be there to serve Sapphire.

Every night without fail I'm lulled to sleep by Sapphire's purring. In the morning, if I wake up and feel that familiar heaviness Sapphire knows exactly what do to. She'll roll on her back and stare at me or chase her tail, and if none of that raises a smile from me she will try her secret weapon: climbing up the curtains. Usually she will get her claws trapped somewhere and then look at me as she sways backwards and forwards helplessly. It's the funniest thing in the world, and of course I have to get up to save her.

So you see not only did Sapphire save my life she continues to save it every day.

In my early adult years I suffered from bouts of intense depression and like Sarah had days when I wanted to escape from the world, hide under my duvet and never come out. Mercifully, changes in my personal and professional life along with time, perhaps the greatest healer of all, helped me pull through. Reading Sarah's letter brought back memories of my dark years and the precious moments of youth I lost. I couldn't help but think that if I had owned a cat the world may not have seemed such a daunting and bleak place.

If I look back at my twenties and my early thirties there was always a sense that something was missing from my life. I thought it was a career so I chased after that and fulfilled many of my goals. I thought it was marriage and family and was fortunate enough to meet my soulmate and have two beautiful children. I thought it was buying a house or driving the right car or wearing the right clothes. I thought it was travelling the world. I thought it was getting fit and healthy. I thought it was studying and acquiring knowledge. Although all these brought great happiness and fulfilment, none of them completely took away the sense of yearning for something that was always there. And then I opened up my home and my heart to two kittens—Max and Merlin—and it felt like I was coming home. It had been over twenty years since I had last shared my life with a cat, and the sense of contentment they have brought me is priceless. Again this may sound weird if you're not a cat lover, but it really does feel as if I've finally found what has been missing from my life all along—cats.

Life savers

It's no surprise at all to me that scientists are now proving what cat owners have always known—that owning a cat can quite literally save lives. Caring for a cat can reduce stress, ease loneliness and fight depression. It can also reduce the risk of heart disease.

> My cats help lower my worryingly high blood pressure. There is nothing like Dee's purring to soothe the tension of a difficult day at work.
>
> Phil

> When I had to recover from major surgery my three Himalayan cats played a huge part in my successful recovery and in lowering my blood pressure. I spent three weeks in bed surrounded by their comfort, warmth and purring, and they rarely left

my side except to eat and use the litter pan. Once I recovered, they found other places to occupy themselves.

Mary

According to a study released in 2008 at the American Stroke Association International Stroke Conference, people who never had a pet cat were 40 per cent more likely to die of a heart attack over the twenty-year study period than cat owners. They were also 30 per cent more likely to die of any cardiovascular disease, including stroke, heart failure and chronic heart disease. The findings emerged from an analysis of data on nearly 4,500 men and women aged thirty to seventy-five who participated in the National Health and Nutrition Examination Study. All were free of cardiovascular disease when they entered the study in the 1970s.

The reasons for these benefits are not fully understood. Part of it may be that cats offer unconditional love and acceptance. It's hard to stay depressed, angry, grumpy or sad when faced with a purring cat! A cat can be your confidant, but never talks back or gives unsolicited advice.

As well as saving lives by helping their owners fight depression and beat the odds of life-threatening conditions, there are also stories, like this one sent to me by Robin, which show that when the situation demands it cats can rescue their owners by, quite literally, jumping in.

THUMPER

I thought you might enjoy reading this story. It's about my cat. We call him Thumper because when he pads his paws up and down he does it in such a rough way it looks like he is thumping. Thumper, a plain old moggie but a pedigree to us, belongs to my seven-year-old son Michael. We gave Thumper to him when he was only two years old and Thumper just seems to know that he belongs to Michael as he reserves his special stares and purrs for him and him alone.

Michael has dangerously low blood sugar levels and we have to be constantly alert. One night about three months ago Thumper woke Michael up in the middle of the night by jumping on his chest. Michael felt a little stunned and frightened at being woken so abruptly so he went into my bedroom and climbed into bed with me. Thumper must have followed Michael into my bedroom because as soon as Michael put his head on my pillow Thumper jumped on his chest again. I can't explain why, but Thumper's unusual behaviour got me worried so I thought I better check Michael's blood pressure. I found out that his blood sugar levels were dangerously low and if Thumper hadn't woken Michael up he would have gone into diabetic shock!

Continuing the theme of jumping cats, Cindy emailed me from Australia to tell me this sweet story about her cat Ollie.

WAKE UP CALL

I've been married to my husband, John, for fifteen years and we sleep in separate bedrooms. This isn't because we have got fed up with each other but because my husband has the loudest snore ever. Even if I sleep in separate rooms with earplugs in I can sometimes still hear him bellowing out. It's a running joke in our family that we need not just separate bedrooms but separate houses in different streets to get a good night's sleep.

When we moved house five years ago I made sure that our bedrooms were as far apart as possible. My cat Ollie—not a girl's name but if you saw her you'd know that it really suits her—a stunning blue and white Siberian, loved our new house 'cause it's four floors high with winding staircases for her to run up and full of places for her to hide. She thinks she is brave and lords—or should that be ladies—it over our dog Stan,

150

but she's actually a real scaredy-cat when visitors call round and you won't see anything of her until they have gone. She's also incredibly vain. I've never seen a cat preen and pamper itself as much as she does. She'll spend hours on her face until it is just right.

You can tell I'm crazy about Ollie 'cause I've been distracted here from the story I have to tell, the story of how Ollie saved my husband's life. What I wanted to tell you is that about two years ago John started complaining to me that Ollie was pestering him at night, jumping on his chest and meowing around his bed. He would put her out of the bedroom and try to go back to sleep but then she would scratch at the bedroom door trying to get in.

My first response was jealousy. I really wanted Ollie to sleep with me at night and not with John. I asked John to come and get me the next time it happened. The following night John came into my bedroom bleary-eyed and handed Ollie to me in a daze and then went back to bed. I kept Ollie in my room that night and she slept under my bed. In the morning I asked John how he was and he told me that even though Ollie hadn't repeatedly woken him he felt like he had been hit over the head by a sledgehammer.

This got me thinking. For a number of years now John seemed to wake up tired, spend the day tired and go to bed tired. His snoring was worse than ever so I decided to make an appointment for him with our doctor to see if he should have a sleep test. A consultant appointment later and John was diagnosed with obstructive sleep apnoea, really severe. I'm not a nurse or doctor and so am quoting here from some of the reference literature we were given about sleep apnoea: 'In obstructive sleep apnoea, a person's airway narrows, or totally collapses, during sleep so that oxygen doesn't reach a person's heart or brain. As a result, a person stops breathing briefly multiple times throughout the night and waking up is the brain's survival mechanism. The person's sleep is interrupted often, which may cause excessive daytime sleepiness or even high blood pressure, significantly increasing the risk of fatal accidents and heart attacks and stroke.'

I can't be sure of this, but I believe that Ollie was waking John when he stopped breathing for periods of time that were dangerous. John is now on medication and has a breathing machine with him that he uses at night. Ollie stays with him every night, and although I still wish she would stay with me, it's comforting knowing that

John is being cared for in such a loving and gentle way.

Tamsin's story, sent to me via email, is similar to Cindy's in that she also believes her cat saved the life of a loved one.

WHISKERS

Whiskers is a very unoriginal name but you'd understand if you saw my cat. She's got a really tiny head but she has this huge pair of long whiskers that seem to drag her down. Everybody who sees them immediately talks about her whiskers and nods their head when I tell them her name.

I've always loved Whiskers dearly but I love her passionately now and I'll tell you why. When my three-year-old daughter Lara got ill with a severe chest infection her doctor seemed to prescribe anything and everything but none of it worked. We were urged to move her to hospital. I was nervous and didn't want to let her go but realized that I had no choice, and arrangements were made for her to leave first thing in the morning if there was no sign of recovery.

The night before she was due to move to hospital I didn't sleep a wink. I sat by my daughter all night, clinging to her hand. She looked so weak and must have lost a good seven pounds since her infection. I was terrified of losing her. I was really scared.

Eventually, it must have been about four or five in the morning, I fell into a deep and heavy sleep. When I opened my eyes a few hours later I could see that Whiskers was lying on Lara's chest. Her purring was so loud it sounded like an engine. I got anxious at first but then I looked at Lara's face. She looked so content and her hand was resting gently on Whiskers' head.

I watched the two of them sleep peacefully like this for about half an hour until Lara started to twitch and mumble. Then Lara opened her eyes and smiled at me. I screamed for my husband, and as soon as he arrived I told him that Lara had got her strength back. We didn't need to take Lara into hospital after all.

For weeks after I wondered if Whiskers had played a part in Lara's recovery or if it was all just coincidence. After a severe migraine attack I made my mind up. When I was a child I used to suffer terribly from migraines and they used to last days. This time the head pains only lasted two hours because when I lay down on my bed Whiskers came up to me, curled into a ball and started purring.

It's not just during illnesses that cats can quite literally be lifesavers; they can also save their owners from life-threatening accidents in the home. I'd like to begin here with an awesome story sent to me by Matilda.

FROSTY, OUR HERO CAT

When I found out I was going to have triplets I was over the moon. I'd been trying for a baby for close to ten years and now three were going to come along all at once. People warned me that it was going to be very tough but I didn't really believe them until my girls arrived, weighing just three pounds. They were so very tiny. It was sure going to be tough.

I did get a lot of help from my family when I was finally able to take the triplets home from hospital. My mum and mum-in-law organized a shift system, with my sister and brother on standby. For the first six months all our lives revolved around the triplets. They were fed every few hours, and the rest of the day was taken up with cleaning, changing and rocking. We tried to put them in the cots for 7 pm every night and sometimes they did all sleep together, but more often than not one or all of them were wide awake. I've never felt so tired and never had any time for myself or to do anything around the house. I really needed a cook, a cleaner and a nanny. Instead I had my family and Frosty, our cat.

Frosty had come as a surprise to us, just like the triplets. I never thought I would own a pet but when we found this kitten abandoned in a cardboard box one day outside our doorstep we just couldn't take her to the RSPCA. We didn't think anyone would want her because she was a bit of mess with spots and spats of white all over her brown and black fur. Over time we grew very fond of her. I was perhaps the one who loved her the most, and during my pregnancy her purring and padding comforted me on many sleepless nights.

When the triplets came home for the first time, Frosty was fascinated by them. I'd done a lot of reading during my pregnancy about the risk of disease and suffocation from cats so I kept them apart. At first I could tell this upset Frosty but she was intelligent and after a few days learned that she wasn't supposed to be around them.

When the triplets were about four months old Frosty disobeyed our strict no-contact-with-the-babies rule. I'm so happy she did because if she hadn't I might not be writing this email to you today. In the last few weeks I had noticed that flowers friends had brought me were dying very quickly, but the triplets kept me so busy I didn't have time to think this through. I'd also been suffering from headaches and serious back pain but thought that was all to do with the stresses and strains of caring for the triplets.

One afternoon I was using the little free time I had to email my friends when all of a sudden Frosty jumped up and sat on my desk. She' d done that many times before so I wasn't worried, so I reached out to stroke her but this time she started to act really odd. She was biting her paws really savagely. I picked her up to see if there was any sign of infection or something wrong with her paws but they looked soft and clean. I put her down on the floor and almost immediately she started to pant loudly with her tongue pushed forward between her teeth. The panting was spasmodic and not constant and it freaked me a bit. Then she jumped onto my keyboard and started to bash at the keys. She seemed really desperate. I didn't know what was wrong so I took her to her cat flap. She rushed outside.

I went back to my computer but a few minutes later I heard a dull thudding noise coming from the nursery monitor. Instinctively I sensed something was wrong so I ran upstairs to the nursery. When I got there I saw that the nursery door was open and Frosty was on the bookcase knocking down books onto the floor. I don't know how the door had opened as we always made a point of closing it. How had Frosty got inside?

I ran into the nursery and tried to grab Frosty, but as I did she made a flying leap from the bookcase into one of the triplets' cots. It was amazing to see her fly like that through the air but now she was sitting on the baby and running around in the crib. It really scared me. I lifted my baby out of the cot to protect her and as I did Frosty jumped out and started to pant and lie down on the floor again.

By now my husband and mum-in-law were in the nursery and they made sure all three babies were all right. I picked Frosty up and took her out of the room. As I did she became really agitated and started to paw the air at an invisible bug. There was clearly something wrong with her so I grabbed my cat cage, put her inside and called the vet.

The vet examined Frosty and gave her an anti-inflammatory shot before asking me if it was possible that Frosty could have been poisoned by cleaning supplies that were left out, or any medications or antifreeze. I said that as far as I knew this wasn't possible, and the vet agreed because Frosty's eyes exhibited normal pupilary response; most household poisons and drugs cause animal pupils to either dilate or contract, or grow sluggish in their response to light. The only other possibility the vet could suggest was carbon monoxide poisoning.

When there is a fire it is not just the flames that cause death but smoke inhalation, specifically carbon monoxide poisoning. Carbon monoxide makes the brain swell by depriving the body and brain of oxygen. The smaller the brain the less brain tissue there is to swell and the smaller the space available to accommodate the swelling. In other words the smaller the human or animal the sooner it will die.

I told my vet that it couldn't be carbon monoxide poisoning because we had a carbon monoxide monitor at home. The vet asked me when I had last checked the batteries. I didn't have a clue; everything had been such a blur since the triplets had been born. I hadn't had time to be efficient and organized about household tasks. I called home to ask my mother-in-law to check. She phoned back and told me that the batteries were dead. I could hear my husband replacing them on the phone. Then I heard the siren wailing and my mum-in-law hastily saying that it was time to get everyone out of the house.

A day later I found out from the gas man that our furnace had a fault and it was pumping out small but toxic amounts of odourless carbon monoxide through the air vents into every room of our home. I was also told that if the weather had turned colder and I had turned the furnace on I would have put my whole family in danger.

If I hadn't taken Frosty to the vet I might never have found out about the furnace and I might not be alive today. I really believe that Frosty behaved in such a strange way that afternoon to force me to take notice of her and do something. We were not in danger that day but if I had turned up the furnace I would have been. Frosty was playing a game of charades with me. She wasn't being affected by the carbon monoxide. She wasn't trying to get fresh air or cool down. She was pretending to be sick. She was trying to warn me. She's one incredible cat.

Frosty is our hero and she is now a fully fledged member of our family. She isn't separated from the triplets any more. She would never do anything to harm them— she is their guardian angel. She saved their lives and our lives. She is the mother of six kittens herself now and we are all helping her as much as we can. I know, perhaps better than anyone, that when it comes to raising a litter of children you can always do with the extra help.

This story isn't as uncommon as you might think. In 2008 the American Society for the Prevention of Cruelty to Animals named Winnie their cat of the year for similar heroic actions. Here, summarized, is her story.

Around 1 am on March 24, 2007, in New Castle, Indiana, a fourteen-year-old cat that belonged to Eric and Cathy Keesling began jumping on their bed, nudging Cathy's ear and meowing loudly. In the words of Cathy, 'It was a crazy meow, almost like screaming.' Cathy didn't get up until Winnie's screaming became persistent, but when she did eventually get out of bed she felt nauseous and faint. Each time she passed out Winnie woke her by screaming again. Cathy couldn't wake her husband so called 911 but couldn't speak. Police traced her call and arrived at the Keeslings' house. Paramedics found the couple's son Michael unconscious on the floor near his bedroom. All the family were treated for carbon monoxide poisoning but soon recovered.

Here's another incredible cat hero story.

161

I've read several of your books and I'm writing to you because I know you won't find it strange when I say that a cat saved my life. It happened over forty years ago now when I was about fourteen. I moved into the basement downstairs and made it into my den. Often I'd sleep there at night too. There were a few problems though because the basement was downhill and it didn't have any drainage so when it rained it could get very damp. One night I fell asleep and in the middle of the night a storm broke out. About three in the morning I was woken up by my cat Toto—and yes, I know that's a really odd name for a cat, but what can I say? I used to love *The Wizard of Oz*! Toto pawed on my chest and seemed distressed so I got up and saw that the room was starting to flood. I banged the ceiling and shouted for Mum and Dad, and they came down and tried to get me out. The water was rising fast and the door was stuck. I was getting scared now.

Dad kept pushing hard against the door but it wouldn't budge. Holding Toto tight I stood on my bed crying. I can't remember much but I do know she licked me a lot. Dad came back with a hammer and started bashing the door but progress was slow.

162

Mum called the emergency services and it must have taken them fifteen minutes to arrive. The water was five foot high by the time they arrived and close to six foot when they finally bashed open the door and pulled me and Toto through. The fire brigade was also on the scene and they were amazed that I was alive as the risk of electric shock was high.

I often think that if Toto hadn't been with me and woken me up that night I would probably not be alive now, as the water would have only have woken me up when it reached me in bed. I don't think there would have been enough time for the emergencies services to get me out.

Sadly, Toto disappeared about six months after he saved my life. I never found him and don't know what happened to him. My mum thinks someone poisoned him. I know that horrible things could have happened to him but I like to think that he went to another home and saved someone's life there.

Firefighters and other heroes

Every so often stories about firefighting cats, like the ones below, appear online or in the press, capturing the public's interest and the hearts of cat lovers all over the world.

According to officials, when a family home in Cairns, north Queensland, Australia caught fire in December 2006 a pet cat scratched the face of its sleeping owner and saved the lives of a family of four. In the words of fire service spokesman Robert White-MacFarlane, 'The cat was probably the best smoke alarm system,' and the house only suffered minor damage. The fire probably started when a mattress caught fire, but before the blaze destroyed the home, 'The occupant was woken by the household cat which was scratching his face, alerting (him) to the ensuing dangers,' Mr White-MacFarlane told the Australian Broadcasting Corporation. After being woken by the cat, the owner was able to wake the rest of the family, leave the house and call the fire service. The house did have smoke alarms but the smoke saturation had not reached a point where they activated the alarms.

BARNEY

In 2006 the Cats Protection League named six-year-old Barney cat of the year after hearing about his courageous actions. In the summer of 2006 Gerald Davies, his wife and twenty-three-year-old son were in bed in their house in Gwersyllt, near Wrexham, Wales when their kitchen cooker caught fire. Barney raced up and down the stairs and made so much noise that he woke everyone up in time for them to leave and alert the fire service. Mr Davies said, 'After what he did, he means everything to us, I think we wouldn't be here now because the smoke in the house that night was unbelievable.'

The following story comes from the *Muskegon News* Archive in the USA.

OREO

In 2008 an entire family asleep in their Allendale home were able to escape flames engulfing their house because they were woken up by the screams of their black and white family cat, Oreo. Diane Busscher was woken up at 4.45 a.m. by the cries of Oreo coming from the garage. When she investigated she saw smoke and flames and rushed back inside to wake up her husband, Warren, and their five children. Lt Michael Keefe suspected that the fire was started by an electrical problem in the garage and the smoke detectors didn't go off until the whole family was out of the house. The fire went on to destroy the entire garage and one of the family bedrooms, causing an estimated $60,000 worth of damage. Keefe said, 'That cat was making a ruckus and, if it didn't, who knows what would have happened.' Jesse Busscher admitted to the *Grand Rapids Press* that most of the family didn't like cats. 'We love it now. This thing is getting some tuna tonight.'

It's brilliant when astonishing stories like these filter into the press and receive the attention they deserve because they encourage others—like Linda, who sent this equally amazing story—to come forward and name their cats as heroes as well.

WELCOME INTRUDER

I'm more of a dog than a cat person but I owe my life to a cat. Earlier this year [2009] I was fast asleep one night on the sofa when this cat woke me up. It was patting my face. My window was open and he must have jumped in that way. As I said I don't like cats so it freaked me out. I picked him up and put him back outside. Feeling unsettled because I'd been woken so abruptly I told the cat in no uncertain terms to clear off and banged the window shut. Looking at my watch I saw that it was close to midnight so I switched the television off, but as soon as I did I heard these strange noises coming from the hallway. I also saw smoke circling around my feet. It was terrifying. I called the fire services immediately.

There's no doubt about it but that cat saved my life. I did have smoke detectors but at the time the downstairs one had run out of batteries. I kept saying to myself that I needed to replace the batteries, but every time I went to the shops I forgot. I have been getting quite forgetful these days. When fire crews arrived it took them about forty-five minutes to beat the flames. The fire started in the kitchen, and if I'd stayed asleep for ten or so minutes longer there's little doubt the levels of smoke would have been fatal.

I haven't really told anyone about the cat jumping in to wake me up. My landlady is allergic to cats and she wouldn't like the idea of a stray wandering the streets and jumping into the house. I'm worried she might set traps down for him, even if I told her my story. I also don't want her to know that my smoke alarm wasn't working. I have a whole new respect for cats now and it would make me so happy if that cat visited me again. It's been several months now but I still keep that window open and a tin of cat food in the cupboard in the hope that he might jump in and I can thank him—or perhaps it was a her—properly.

Linda discovered that when human lives are at stake cats are willing to step forward and help even those who don't care much for them—or in Wayne's case those who can't always hear or see them.

SEVEN LIVES

I'm deaf and partially sighted, but thanks to my cat Seven I'm not dead. One afternoon I was resting in my bedroom with Seven sleeping beside me. I was taking a nap when all of a sudden Seven jumped onto my chest and dug his claws into me. She wasn't a vicious cat and this was very strange. I got up rubbing my chest as the scratches felt itchy and sore. When I got up the aroma of smoke was strong. I opened my bedroom door and could smell burning coming from the kitchen.

I went to the kitchen to check for fire but everything seemed fine. I thought it must have been the neighbours having a barbecue or something so I went back to my bedroom. When I got there Seven started to tug at my feet. I was worried I would step on him. I couldn't be angry with him though as he is my best friend and hadn't done this before. I went back to the kitchen with Seven rushing ahead of me. I thought he was eager for food but he didn't

168

go into the kitchen and just stood in front of the door. My sight isn't brilliant but I saw a reflection of what might have been flames on the kitchen wall. Later I found out that a fire on the stove had caused my kitchen to burst into flames. I grabbed the fire extinguisher and pointed it in the direction of the stove but what I didn't know was that the smoke was going over the stove cover and filling my house fast.

Struggling to breathe, I grabbed Seven and left my house to call the fire services. One of the firefighters told me that my kitchen would have gone up in flames before the smoke alarm went off. So if Seven hadn't warned me and I'd settled down for a nap in my bedroom as I had planned I might have died.

Every day Seven helps me cope with my disabilities. He is my ears and my eyes and my heart. I am so grateful to him. He's more than a cat and more than a best friend. He's my angel cat.

Cats can certainly show remarkable courage when it comes to warning their owners about potentially life-threatening fires. What is interesting, as the story below from the *New York Daily News* illustrates, is that they can show the same fierce courage when it comes to defending their young, suggesting to me that the bond between cat and owner may be as powerful and as instinctive as that of a mother to its young. Could it be then that we owners have got it wrong when we think that our cats regard us as their surrogate parents? Do they perhaps think of us as their surrogate children in need of love and protection?

ALL ABOUT SCARLETT

In 1996 a remarkable calico cat named Scarlett risked her life to save her kittens from a burning building. When an abandoned garage in Brooklyn caught fire one day the stray cat and her four-week-old babies that had been living there survived. When firefighters arrived to put out the fire they found a badly burned Scarlett carrying her kittens out one by one from the burning building. She saved all five kittens, collapsing with pain and exhaustion on the floor.

Scarlett and her kittens were taken to a local animal rescue league, and with the exception of one kitten that died of a virus, were all adopted into loving homes. Scarlett passed away in 2008 but she left a huge impression on her owner Karen Wellen, who is quoted as saying, 'She was the most precious and loving cat, and in our household, it was all about Scarlett.'

Scarlett's story attracted worldwide media

attention at the time and over 7,000 people asked to adopt her. The legacy she left behind her is as impressive as her life had been. The North Shore Animal League of America created the Scarlett Award for Animal Heroism in her honour. This is presented to animals that have performed heroic acts to benefit others, whether humans or animals.

*   *   *

Fire isn't the only danger that cats have faced to save lives. Although I haven't had a personal account sent to me I have read stories online about cats taking the bite of a deadly snake for their owners or their young and sometimes paying the ultimate price for their courage. To defend the ones they love they will even face up to their arch-enemies, as Rob, who sent me this story a few weeks ago, explains.

KILLER INSTINCT

Everyone thinks my lovely cat Jinx is very independent and fierce but I know him better. When he's alone with me, he's a big soft baby. I have to admit though that he is a killer and will spend days hunting, returning with gifts of birds or mice for me. Mercifully, the animals are always dead and I never see him play with them. I couldn't stomach that.

171

Living next door but one to us is a man who owns a very vicious Staffordshire terrier. I don't think he treats it very well because it is always straining at the leash and looks half crazed. All the kids in the street, me included, are frightened of it. I'm seventeen now but this beast still scares the life out of me. I have never seen such a frightening dog.

I can remember when I was about ten years old Mum asked me to buy some newspapers from the corner shop. When I went outside I saw Jinx, who was only about three then, playing with something in the grass. I could hear the dog barking as I passed its house. I noticed that it was tied up so I stuck my tongue out at it. I went to the shop and bought the paper and then started to walk back home. I heard the familiar barking but this time it was even more vicious than ever. Somehow as I walked past the dog got loose and raced towards me. I froze in fear.

It must have only been for a few seconds but time didn't move. Everything went into slow motion. I thought it best not to run away as this might make it worse so I just stood still and avoided eye contact hoping it would pass me by. I knew that if it was set on attacking me I was toast. I was like a rabbit caught in the headlights.

Then the most amazing thing happened.

Little Jinx appeared in front of me. His little body was so puffed up that he looked twice the size and rather scary himself. I didn't know that cats' tails can get so big. Jinx stood in front of me hissing, and then as the dog approached jumped at it scratching at its face. I don't think the dog had ever encountered such an angry cat before and turned away whimpering.

So there you have it: Jinx saved my life. My neighbour made sure that his dog never got loose again and I made sure— and continue to make sure—that Jinx always has some milk when he returns home in the morning from a busy night's hunting.

Evie's story is similar to Rob's because it also shows that when their owners are in danger cats are prepared to go that extra mile and, if need be, change their behaviour or act out of character.

CAT BURGLAR

India is my rag-doll indoor cat. I adopted her fifteen years ago when she was seriously ill and paid for the vet care that saved her life. It was one of the best decisions I ever made. Coming home to her purrs and unconditional love is the highlight of every day. I live alone but with

India in residence I never feel lonely.

I live in a one-bedroom ground-floor flat on a busy street so I can't let India out. The area where I live has a high population of cats and she is so timid she wouldn't stand a chance. I want her to be happy so I spend as much time as I can playing and cuddling with her. It's often hard to tear myself away from her when she is in one of her really affectionate moods. She was in one of those moods one Sunday afternoon. I'd just got home from doing my weekly grocery shop and when I came into my living room I found India dozing in the sunshine. I gave her a stroke and she immediately started purring and rolling on her back.

I wanted to stay with her a while longer but I had a lot of things to do. I opened my window to let some fresh air in and as a compromise stroked her a little, and then did some chores, returned to stroke her and did another chore and so on. I didn't leave her alone for more than a few minutes, but what I didn't realize is that is how long it takes for someone to quietly put their hand through the open window, slide it right down and step inside. Before this happened I was watching India play with a tiny piece of string—one of her favourite games—when I remembered that I hadn't put fresh sheets on my bed and I went to my bedroom to remake my bed. Within a minute India came chasing after me without her piece of string.

I had never seen India run as fast since she was a kitten. She's quite an old cat now and suffers from arthritis and so her movements are typically slow. She started to swirl around my feet and the fast movements must clearly have hurt her. I knew then that something must be wrong. She was also making the sickest meow sound from her twelve-pound body, sounds I had never heard her make. She was like a wild cat. She was telling me that something malevolent was in my flat. Shaking with fear, I peered out of my bedroom door and saw a man with a stocking pulled over his face in my kitchen. I screamed and locked my bedroom door. The screams didn't stop there; they kept on coming and each one was louder than the last. Like India I had discovered a voice I didn't know I had. Somehow amid all that screaming I had the good sense to grab my panic button and push it several times.

By the time the police arrived the man had fled but not before he had taken several hundred pounds-worth of stuff from my living room. My description of the burglar matched that of a notorious and violent burglar the police had been trying to catch in my area for months. The police told me I was fortunate that my cat had given me a warning because he would have shown me no mercy if I hadn't been able to lock myself in the bedroom and frightened him with my screams.

Over the years that I've had India my neighbours and friends have often laughed at me for the time and money I have spent on her, but they don't laugh now, and all that time and love hasn't been wasted. I saved India's life and now she has saved me. India may also have helped saved the lives of other residents in my street too because once news spread of the break-in to my apartment new security measures were put in place not just for my flat but for many others.

Many people believe that cats have a highly developed intuition or sixth sense and can warn us when we are in danger, and in my years of paranormal research and writing there hasn't been any lack of stories about this phenomenon. But it's not just by warning their owners of danger that cats can save lives; they can also intervene more directly, as the following two stories I stumbled upon illustrate so well. The first comes from Pawprints and Paws Inc. in Louisiana, USA, and the second appeared on ABC News Online on 17 April 2006.

One bitterly cold night in January the life of Nina Sweeney from Lawrence, Massachusetts, USA was saved by her seven cats and one dog. The temperature had fallen dramatically when she went to bed and it was bitterly cold. Sometime during the night Nina was rendered helpless when a paralysing illness took hold of her. She couldn't get out of bed when her fire went out. Before long the house was freezing as temperatures outside registered well below zero. Nina lived alone and it would be two days before neighbours suspected something was wrong because they hadn't seen her out and about. When they eventually reached her she was very hungry but alive and warm because there were cats on either side of her, on her chest, under her arm and another draped around her neck. Two other cats and her dog were lying on her stomach. Nina's seven cats and one dog had saved her from a very cold death.

THE CAT IS A HERO

According to police spokesman Uwe Beier, in April 2006 the life of a newborn baby abandoned on the doorsteps of a Cologne house in Germany in the middle of the night was saved by a cat meowing loudly until someone woke up. In the words of Beier, 'The cat is a hero. Its loud meowing got the attention of the homeowner and saved the baby from suffering life-threatening hypothermia. The homeowner opened the door to see why the cat was making so much noise and discovered the newborn.'

Mr Beier went on to say that the baby boy was taken to hospital at 5.00 am local time when overnight temperatures fell towards zero and had only suffered mild hypothermia.

Both these stories are powerful and beautiful examples of the awesome strength of the cat–human bond. They can be our best friends and our most devoted champions.

* * *

Before moving on to the next chapter, where you'll read incredible stories about cats using their sixth sense to predict natural disasters or locate their owners even when they are several hundred miles apart, I'd like to close with this fantastic hero-cat story sent to me from Canada by Jon. I think you'll like it, because I haven't met a cat lover yet who didn't.

This happened back in the 1980s. I had this calico cat called Tobias and he was such a personality. I've had cats since and each one is great in their own way but Tobias was a once-in-a-lifetime kind of cat. The way he used to look at me was really as if he could read my mind, and that's how he earned his name. Originally we called him Smokey but then I read this book at school called *Tobias the Magic Cat* and it just seemed to suit him so I changed his name to Tobias.

Anyway, I need to tell you what he did and why I am emailing you. One night Tobias was sleeping on my bed when he heard faint sounds coming from the kitchen window being opened. He must have sensed that something wasn't right, or perhaps he didn't like the squeak the window was making, or perhaps he didn't like the cold air coming in, or perhaps he didn't like the smell of the strange person trying to get inside his house. Either way he jumped up, howled with rage, puffed his body up twice its normal size and rushed to face the enemy.

Tobias's howl woke me up instantly and curious to know what was going on I went into the kitchen. The image I saw there will never leave me. It was just incredible. I saw a man's leg and upper body easing itself into the kitchen, and as soon as a face with a black hat pulled over it emerged Tobias leapt into action. He jumped right onto his face and tore at it. The burglar clearly wasn't prepared for a savage cat and fell backwards out of the window. I ran over to take a look as our kitchen window is fairly high up, and I saw him lying there with the ladder he had used to climb up lying across his body. He was howling with pain. There was blood on his face and he was clutching his leg. He must have strained or broken something.

On the windowsill was a boot but he didn't appear to notice it was missing. Tobias had frightened him so much that all he could think about was getting away. It didn't take long for the police to catch up with a limping one-booted burglar, and he was in a prison cell that very night. The best part of this story and what makes me smile the most is that when questioned the burglar told police that in his crime spree—which spanned nearly ten years until he was caught out by Tobias—he made a point of avoiding houses with dogs. By underestimating the cleverness and power of the domestic cat, he made, in the words of my screen hero, one big mistake!

6. Cat Sense

Always the cat remains a little beyond the limits we try to set for him in our blind folly.

Andre Norton

Stories of cats with remarkable abilities to predict natural disasters or weather changes abound. Most of these are about cats acting strangely before an earthquake, flood or savage storm, but there are also stories about cats predicting man-made disasters such as bombs, explosions or air raids. During World War II many households discovered that their cat was a more reliable early-warning system than the sirens.

I've had several letters from cat lovers informing me that their cat sensed an earthquake before it happened. Tony's story is fairly typical. Here in his own words he describes the bizarre behaviour of his cat Widget.

MILES AWAY

I don't know if cats are psychic or anything but what I do know is that my cat Widget—rhymes with fidget because she never stands still—woke me one night. She wailed in my ear and purred so loud and pushed her head into my face. She seemed really frightened and I didn't understand why because it was very quiet outside. Eventually she settled down and slept beside me on my pillow. The next morning as I was listening to the radio while getting dressed I heard that there had been an earthquake in Birmingham and the scientists had detected tremors as far away as London. I'm convinced it was the earthquake that Widget was warning me about. She wasn't to know that it was miles away.

I'm sure you will agree that Miranda's story, below, is breathtaking.

IN A FRENZY

This happened about half an hour before the great North Ridge Earthquake in California in January 1994. My four-year-old daughter Amy was sleeping soundly and I was asleep with my husband. It was the middle of the night.

At the time we had a kitten—she must have been about ten months old, I think—and she used to sleep every night with my daughter. Amy told me later that Kitten (we hadn't given her a name yet, somehow Kitten just suited her) woke her up by

182

jumping off her bed and racing around her bedroom in a frenzy. Amy sat up to see what was going on and Kitten leapt back on the bed and started to bite her hair. She did everything she could to make Amy get out of bed and come to us. As soon as Amy had woken us up, Kitten calmed down, although she did keep meowing in a very strange way. We hadn't spayed her yet so we wondered if she could be on heat and were just about to go back to bed when the ground started to shake and roll about. We hid under the kitchen table and clung together as we heard windows breaking and the ceiling cracking. I said my prayers over and over again. My daughter clutched Kitten really tight but she didn't make a sound. I think she was as frightened as us. Then we heard water sloshing about around us. We used to have a pool outside in our yard. It must have broken up too.

It was an ordeal and one I hope to never see happen to us again but the important thing is that we survived. We might not have though if Kitten—we finally named her Lourdes, because she was our miracle—had not woken us up and got us all together in the kitchen—the part of our home that experienced the least damage. Thanks to Lourdes we were not unprepared as sadly many others were.

These stories share similarities to others I've heard or read about cats, and I quote the typical phrases used: 'freaking out' , 'acting strangely' , 'howling in our ears' or in some cases 'simply disappearing' . They would come as no surprise to cat historians and experts as the phenomenon has been reported for centuries.

Another frequently reported phenomenon is cats that appear to be able to predict the weather, in particular violent storms. Here's Trudy's story.

FALLING DOWN

This happened a while ago now but I remember it as clear as if it happened yesterday. My mum and dad had come down to visit me. We'd just finished eating supper when my cat Camilla started to pull and tear at the curtains. Usually when Camilla does this I tell her off and she goes away, but this time she ignored me and kept on going back, and each time she got back to the curtains she got more and more insistent with the tearing. Soon my curtains would be in shreds, so I scolded her, picked her up and locked her in the hall, but she clawed and clawed at the living-room door.

We all did our best to ignore the clawing but it was impossible. Besides my mum and dad were cat lovers like me, and I could tell it was distressing them so eventually I opened the door. Camilla rushed back inside and hid behind the sofa. I couldn't stay angry with her for long and soon forgot about her behaviour as I chatted more with Mum and Dad.

When it was time for them to drive home I walked with them into the hall and Camilla followed. I nearly tripped up over her. Then she jumped up onto one of my indoor plants—my pride and joy—and pulled it down crashing to the floor. There was mud everywhere and the pot had shattered into several pieces. I was too upset about all the mess and the loss of my plant to scream at Camilla, who must have scampered away. Mum and Dad took their coats off and helped me pick up everything. It took us a good half an hour to clear everything away. Then when they finally got out of the door I noticed it had suddenly got very dark outside. I also saw flashes of thunder in the distance. Dad's vision wasn't as good as it should be and I was worried about him. The lightning was good enough warning for me. I didn't want them driving down dark, winding country roads in this weather and I made them stay the night.

The next day we heard that the storm had an air pressure equal to a category 3 hurricane. During the night countless trees had fallen and over twenty people had died. I'm just so glad Mum and Dad weren't driving back in the dark that night. If Camilla hadn't destroyed my plant there's no telling what might have happened if they had set off. All this happened in 1987 and seems a long time ago now. Both my parents and Camilla have passed away and this may sound silly but it comforts me to know that they are all together—somewhere.

Other stories tell of mother cats moving their kittens from an area or house which is later destroyed by flood or a landslide to a safer refuge. The sheer volume of such stories suggests that cats most definitely have an ability to predict natural disasters. The question scientists are asking is: how do they do it?

There are several theories as to how cats can predict natural disasters. They could be able to detect changes in static electricity. Experts believe that changes in the earth's magnetic fields produce alterations in static electricity and cats can sense these. Cats will only sleep in places that they feel are safe. So in this way a domestic cat may help people seek out places of safety. During rainstorms huge amounts of electricity are discharged into the clouds, creating electromagnetic waves that spread into the atmosphere for several hundred miles. The air becomes charged with positive ions, which some believe may influence the concentration of chemicals in the brain. This could perhaps explain why some people experience headaches before thunderstorms. Cats may be extremely sensitive to these ions, and chemical changes within their brains could explain their mood and behaviour changes.

A cat's nostrils may also play an important part in its powers of prediction. A cat's sense of smell is fourteen times stronger than a human's, and it uses scent to detect food, friends, foes and territory which has been marked. (I remember once visiting a litter of kittens barely ten or so days old and when I crouched down and placed my hand near one kitten's nose he hissed at me. His eyes looked like they were still closed but his powerful sense of smell was already developed enough to warn him of potential danger.) A cat's nose along with its powerful accessory, the Jacobson's organ—located inside the mouth just behind the front teeth, and connected to the nasal cavity—could therefore act as an early-warning system. When a cat opens its mouth the Jacobson's organ connects via ducts to the nasal cavity—when a cat does this it often looks like it is smiling, although to others it is a grimace. Cats perhaps use their Jacobson's organ to sample molecules in dilute concentrations in the air and get an early warning of more disturbing changes to come— such as when a volcano starts to smoke and release gases.

A cat's hearing is also far superior to that of a human. Some cats rub their ears before a rainstorm and it is conceivable that they are responding to pressure changes that irritate their sensitive inner ears. Or maybe they can hear the screams from those at the epicentre? Another theory suggests that cats are super-sensitive to underground vibrations. The extreme sensitivity of their feet and whiskers could help them pick up the tiny tremors that precede an earthquake.

Taking into account cats' sensitivity to vibrations, their superior sense of smell and their ability to hear ultrasonic sounds that detect magnetic changes, it is possible to conclude that an impending earthquake or storm might manifest as loud and clear to a cat as an air raid siren, and could very probably be detected by a cat in this subtle form several hours before we humans become aware of it. This explanation is rational and persuasive, and almost convinces me, but then I receive letters like this one sent by Shirley, who lives in London, and it doesn't seem as persuasive. I'm not sure how scientists could explain this one.

Every morning I leave my flat in King's Cross at the same time, grab a Starbucks and a paper before catching the Tube to work. One morning my clockwork routine was disrupted by my normally very well behaved and independent-minded cat Snoopy. As usual I fed him and chatted with him as I got ready for work, but when I put my coat on and grabbed my briefcase he started to get very vocal. I didn't know he had such a fine pair of lungs. He meowed and purred, and if he hadn't been a neutered male I would have thought he was looking for a female to mate with. It was obvious that he wanted attention. He's normally so independent and not a 'cuddle me' cat, so this did take me by surprise.

I love Snoops dearly so I decided to relax a little that morning and indulge him. I put work second. Even though I had an important meeting I figured it would be okay if I was a few minutes late. I sent a text to my PA and told her that I was going to be a little later than usual that morning. I must have spent about twenty minutes petting my cat, and when he started to get sleepy I put him in his basket and headed for the door. I nearly tripped up as he immediately got up from his basket and started to run in and out of my legs. I had no idea what was the matter with him.

Eventually I managed to edge my way out of the door. It took a while though as Snoops is an indoor cat and he was seriously trying to escape—something he has rarely done before. He only tries to escape when I need to do the hoovering. I was a good thirty minutes late so I realized I needed to make up time. Forgoing my paper and my coffee I started to walk briskly towards the Tube station. Just as I was approaching I was nearly knocked down by a huge crowd of people coming up the stairs. Many were shouting and screaming, and I could sense the panic and confusion. It was the panic and confusion caused by the 7/7 London bombings on the Underground, the Underground that I could well have been on if my cat had not changed my normal routine. I still get tearful when I think how close I was to death or injury that day.

What is incredible about this story is that the cat's behaviour can't be explained by a superior sense of hearing or smell or sensitivity to changes in the environment, as this wasn't a natural but a man-made disaster. On that morning Shirley followed her heart and not her watch and this may just have saved her life. Snoopy has not behaved in this way before or since. A friend of mine had a similar story to tell me about someone he knew who told him that if it hadn't been for the bizarre behaviour of her cat on the morning of 7/7, disrupting her normal routine and making her late, she would almost definitely have been on the number 30 bus that exploded. In fact, she was actually running towards it when the explosion went off.

There is always the argument that Shirley's cat acting strangely on the morning of 7/7 was just an extreme coincidence, but what a magnificent coincidence! Having lived with cats and read stories like this I believe that cats do have a way of sensing things that we cannot. It may well have something to do with their superior senses of sight, hearing and smell, but stories like Shirley's and this one sent to me by Mary certainly suggest something more.

BACKSEAT DRIVER

Whenever I remember or tell this story it still sends shivers down my spine. It happened sixteen years ago when my son was seventeen and eager to own a motorbike of his own. I was dead set against it and refused to even consider the idea. Things got really difficult for me when his best friend was allowed to have a motorbike and my son started hitching rides with him. What could I do? I couldn't stop him so I just begged him to wear a helmet.

One night the friend came round to pick my son up for something, I don't know what—perhaps it was a party or a film. Reluctantly I invited the young man in and called up to my son, who was getting ready upstairs. I was relieved to see that at least the friend had remembered to bring an extra helmet. When my son came downstairs the phone rang and it was his girlfriend, so my son chatted for a few minutes while his friend put the helmets and his jacket down and sat on the sofa waiting.

Eventually, phone call over, my son put on his jacket and grabbed his helmet. What happened then was totally crazy. My son threw the helmet down on the floor and shouted obscenities. It turned out that our cat Darcy had taken a dump in the helmet. This was madness as in all the years we had had her—eight to be precise—she had never once gone to the toilet in the house. The faeces looked quite unpleasant and runny and it was clear that even if the helmet was cleaned my son wasn't going to use it. He said he was going to go without the helmet. Well, this wasn't going to happen as far as I was concerned, so in the end my son was left alone with me in the house while his friend drove away. You could have cut the atmosphere with a knife. I think my son hated me at that moment.

He didn't hate me the next morning when we heard the most distressing news. His friend had been involved in a head-on collision with a truck. He wasn't killed but had broken his legs, several ribs and an arm. Fortunately, because he was wearing his helmet he did not have any head injuries, but just imagine what might have happened to my son if he had been on the back of that bike without a helmet? I don't even want to think about it.

As for Darcy, her bowel movements were completely normal the following morning and she never used the house or someone's helmet as a restroom again. I'm writing to you about this because, as ridiculous as it sounds, I can't help thinking that Darcy was protecting my son. They were very close when he was growing up. Darcy used to sleep with him most nights. Did she know that I wouldn't let him out without a helmet on?

I included Mary's story because I think it illustrates how cats can sometimes communicate their love, compassion and wisdom to their owners in the most surprising ways. Jean would almost certainly agree with this.

I didn't think my ginger cat Topsy liked me that much. I got him from a shelter when he was two years old and I think he had been badly treated because he used to shake all over when people came near him. I knew it was going to take a lot to win his trust. When I first brought him home he shot under my bookcase and wouldn't come out. I didn't try to force him out; I just let him take his time. I was retired and I had plenty of time.

It took several months before Topsy finally started to get more confident around me. One night I was sitting reading when I heard him jump on the back of my chair. I kept absolutely still so he wouldn't get scared but couldn't resist turning round to say hello. Our eyes met briefly and then he shot back under the bed. This went on for a number of weeks and each time Topsy lingered longer with me. Several years later he was still a nervous, jumpy cat (that's why I call him Topsy, as in topsy-turvy) and I'd given up hoping that he would sleep on my lap, but he didn't hide from me any more and would sometimes purr when I talked to him. It took time but I prided myself on the understanding we had built up together.

I was soon to discover just how strong this understanding was. For the past year Topsy would wait until I was settled and then jump onto the bottom of my bed and go to sleep himself. He just watches and waits until I am ready to turn in, but last night he abandoned his usual routine and started acting in a really bizarre way. He jumped on my bed before I had got in it, circled around and around and then jumped back off again. It was like he was trying to tell me something or wanted me to understand something. He kept jumping on and off the bed over and over again. He was really frantic. I tried to calm him down with gentle words but nothing I said or did seemed to help. I was getting tired by now so I undressed and got into bed. It was impossible to sleep because Topsy was making so much commotion.

I got up, and as I did I started to feel shaky and sweaty and dizzy. Then it hit me. I had forgotten to check my blood sugar levels before I went to bed. I'm a diabetic you see and have to be very careful. I'm organized and efficient about self-monitoring my condition most of the time but I'm a movie fan and that night *Titanic* was on and I had got so lost in the story that I had completely forgotten. When I did my glucose test it had fallen dangerously low. If I'd fallen asleep I could have lost consciousness or even died. I wouldn't have made it through the night.

I still get chills down my spine when I think about what happened. How did Topsy know something was wrong? I thank my lucky stars every day that Topsy is in my life. He is my best friend and my caretaker. He may not jump on my lap or pester me for attention like many cats do but he communicates his love and gratitude to me in his own special way.

Jean's wonderful story could easily have slotted into the cat angels or heroes chapters, but I feel that it sits best here because it is a fantastic example of 'cat sense' at work. And while we are on this subject and how scientific explanations of cats' superior sight, hearing, taste and smell are often woefully inadequate to explain stories like those sent to me by Jean, it's important to point out that cats don't only use their psychic powers to protect their owners. They use them to protect themselves as well. To illustrate this, try to think back to the last time you took your cat to the vet. Did your cat disappear or hide when you started to think about getting him or her ready? Cats are notorious for being able to sense when a visit to the vet is in the air.

Animal behaviour expert Rupert Sheldrake, author of *Dogs That Know When Their Owners Are Coming Home*, contacted sixty-five veterinary offices in London and asked if they had noticed cat owners having problems bringing their cats in for appointments. Sixty-four said they had, and some were not even making appointments for cats any more, preferring the owners to come in on a first-come-first-served basis, explaining, 'Cat appointments don't work.' This isn't just because cats notice when their owners get out the cage; cats are known to hide as soon as they sense their owners are starting to think about getting to the vets in time. Again, how do cats know? Is it possible that they are reading their owner's minds?

Alpha beta

A fascinating thing I learned while researching this book which may go some way towards explaining the psychic powers of cats is that the brains of cats fall very naturally into the alpha brainwave state. Humans are normally in the beta state when awake, but when we are relaxed or meditating our brains generate alpha waves, which as any paranormal expert will tell you give access to your subconscious, deeper intuition or sixth sense, call it what you will. In this alpha wave state you are relaxed but also receptive and hyper-alert, so a sudden noise will startle you. Maybe this is why cats that appear to be asleep often freak out when they hear sudden noises or movements. It may also explain why in their consistently relaxed but alert state cats are perhaps able to pick up on their owner's thoughts and feelings.

All this is just speculation, and the psychic powers of cats can't be proved scientifically, but for cat owners who have personal experience of their cat's telepathic and psychic powers no proof is necessary. Nothing has the power of their experience and conviction. I couldn't think of a better place to include Susie's email than here.

PRINCESS AND FELIX

I'm a long-time cat owner and cat lover and I'm 100 per cent convinced that there is more to cats than most people think. They are very perceptive and intelligent. There's nothing lazy about them. Even when they are napping or sleeping their minds stay active and sharp. My late Princess could always tell when there was a thunderstorm coming. She was terrified of thunder and used to pace up and down the room frantically. She could also judge my mood and sensed immediately when I didn't feel well. One time I lay down with this horrible headache. I woke up a few hours later and Princess was sitting on my pillow. Neatly arranged around my head were some mice; she brought them to me to make me feel better. They were a gift.

The cat I own now—Felix—is a real diva. If he wants my attention and I'm talking on the phone he will stand on the phone and disconnect me. He wakes me up without fail at 7 am every morning—even when the clocks change—and sends thoughts to me when he wants to go out or eat. I get this feeling he is outside the door, and when I open it he is there. Like Princess, if I feel sick or sad he will curl up beside me. Without a doubt there is more to a cat than meets the eye.

Susie is convinced that not just her cats but all cats have awesome psychic powers and that if there is a strong bond between owner and cat, humans can benefit a great deal from this.

Incredible journeys

Perhaps no stories better illustrate the strength of the bond between cat and owner and the extraordinary powers that cats have than those of lost cats that have been able to find their owners over great distances, sometimes in places that they have never been to before. One such story concerned a cat whose owners were preparing to move to a new house several hundred miles away. When the day of the move came the cat somehow got left behind but weeks later turned up at the new house. How this cat was able to work out the right direction to take or find its owners when they were so far away is a real mystery. But this is not uncommon. There are a number of similar stories and some have become very well known like the story of Sugar, which I related in the Introduction to this book. Other stories are less famous, or not known by anyone at all outside the family, but this doesn't make them any the less remarkable. Jordan was kind enough to send me the story of his cat's incredible journey.

TOM

I lost Tom my orange tabby last September. I was working late so I asked my brother to pick him up from the vet. I don't think my brother secured the cage properly because he managed to escape when my brother left the cage just for a brief moment next to his car. I live about three and a half miles from the vet and I'd only ever taken Tom there by car.

This happened on a Friday and I spent most of Saturday putting up posters about Tom asking if anyone had seen him. He was microchipped so I really hoped he would be found soon. I got a couple of calls from people who thought they saw this bright orange tabby but nothing definite. Then the following Tuesday when I was making breakfast in walks Tom with his tail held high and this defiant look. I just couldn't believe it. He found his way back.

Dorothy's cat Cheetah found her way home in a different sort of way.

NO PLACE LIKE HOME

Cheetah's an indoor cat and two years ago she snuck out of my house when the postman arrived with a delivery. She didn't have any identification tags and had never been out before so I was really worried. For weeks I stood outside banging her food tray, hoping she would come back, but she never did. I worried that I would never see her again but deep down I knew she was out there somewhere, safe and happy.

Five months later I was doing my usual round of visits—I'm a health care worker—when I called in on a woman who had given birth to her fifth child. She was prone to post-natal depression and I just wanted to keep an eye on her. To cut a long story short, when I went into her living room and sat down to talk to her who did I see but Cheetah, sprawled out on the sofa.

There was no mistaking that it was Cheetah because of her distinctive markings. She looked fine and healthy and very content. I didn't know what to say so I asked the woman where she had got her cat. She told me that she had simply turned up at her doorstep one day. She said that she loved the cat dearly and that having her around had really helped her cope since her latest baby was born.

We get to the strange part of the story now. This woman had the same name as me, Dorothy. I never told Dorothy that Cheetah was in fact mine and I decided to let her stay there. She had clearly found the home that was right for her.

Scientists have made great progress in recent years unveiling the mystery of the world of cats, but even though some answers have been found, namely that cats have superior visual memory, hearing, sight and smell, these observations have a habit of raising even more questions. For example, the visual memory of cats can only be a navigational device in areas where they have already been. So how do cats find their way to areas they have never been and sometimes hundreds of miles away? Perhaps cats have an inbuilt magnetic sensitivity which gives them the same homing ability as pigeons or perhaps they can read the geomagnetic patterns on the earth's surface or perhaps they really do have a psychic powers?

In addition to their remarkable navigational powers cats also appear to have an unexplained ability to anticipate the return of their owners, even when the person returns at an unpredictable time and without warning. The 'meet and greet phenomenon' is one that many cat owners spoke to me about when writing this book. Here's a random snapshot of comments from some of the emails I received.

It's like he can sense when I'm walking down the drive.

Grace

As soon as I put my key in the door, there she is beside me welcoming me with purrs and leg rubs.

Rory

My husband tells me that my cat can even sense when it is me on the phone. Sheba will jump onto the window sill expecting to see me.

Tina

I'm self-employed and work irregular hours so I have no idea how my cat knows when I am on my way home but there she is sitting by the front door waiting for me. My wife tells me that when Miss Piggy, my cat, gets up and sits looking out the front-door window I'm usually about twenty to thirty minutes away from me coming home. How does she do it?

Finn

My cat Boots is a loveable rogue. He's always there when I came home, making me forget about the day's worries and strains and eager to be entertained and petted. I don't know what I would do without him. He makes coming home such a joy.

Eve

This 'coming home as one of the highlights of the day' theme cropped up time and time again when I talked to people about their cats and the subject matter of this book. For many cat owners no further proof of the psychic powers of cats is needed than being greeted with unashamed enthusiasm by an animal that is so tuned into you it is somehow able to anticipate your arrival without obvious clues. Can there be any closer bond than that?

I'd like to conclude this chapter with the well-known story of the lion from Harrods. It's a moving and wonderful commentary on one of the central themes of this chapter and indeed this whole book: the remarkable bond that can be established between human and cat, even if that cat is a very large and dangerous one! This comes from *Christian the Lion* by Anthony Bourke and John Rendall.

In the swinging 1960s two Australians, John Rendall and Ace Bourke, purchased a lion cub from the exotic animals department at Harrods. They called it Christian and it travelled around London by Bentley, ate at flash restaurants and spent its days lounging around a King's Road furniture shop and romping through the graveyard at a neighbourhood church.

Over time Christian grew into a hundred-kilo adult lion and needed to be returned to the African wilds. A year later Rendall and Bourke wanted to visit Christian but were told that he was now king of the pride, completely wild and would not remember them. Undaunted, they decided to visit him anyway.

After several hours watching and waiting, Christian recognized his former owners and greeted them with love and enthusiasm. The filmed reunion between Rendall, Bourke and Christian at a game park near Nairobi became an overnight YouTube sensation and touched the hearts of more than forty-four million people.

7. Angel Cats

Cats come and go without ever leaving.
                                    Martha Curtis

Even those who believe in an afterlife for humans may be dismissive of animal ghosts or spirits. It is often said that animals don't have souls or spirits so cannot survive death as humans may do, but animals are made of the same energy as humans, and to my mind there is no reason why they may not survive in the same way. Anyone who has bonded with their cat will be aware of the strong sometimes psychic connection that can exist between human and feline. Psychic and spiritual energy may be aspects of the same phenomenon, so cats could have as much connection to the world of spirit as humans. Perhaps more so, given their superior senses of taste, smell, sight and hearing and their ability to sense what is unseen.

Cats may not only return as ghosts—more about this surprisingly commonly reported phenomenon later—they may also be able to see or sense spirits. Debbie certainly believes that her cat can see ghosts—here's her chilling story.

When I moved to London last year I adopted Sammy, a stray ginger tom. I lived in an old Victorian detached house. It had a rich and colourful history but no accounts as far as I knew of haunting or strange phenomena but within a week of Sammy settling in with me it was like he could see things I could not. He would sit looking at this wall outside my office and his eyes would stare at one particular spot close to the ceiling for ages. He would sit at the bottom of the stairs and his eyes would slowly rise from the bottom step to the top as if someone was walking there.

One evening when I'd closed up my office for the night and settled down in front of the TV I heard this loud thump coming from my office. It was really loud and Sammy jumped up from his sleep and started to act crazy. He ran to my office door and started to scratch at it. I heard another thud from inside. That was enough for me. I grabbed Sammy and ran outside. I suspected intruders and called the police. When they arrived and took a look inside there was nobody inside my office or my house and no signs of forced entry. No picture had fallen and nothing was out of place in my office and I have no idea what caused the loud sound I heard. I think the only one who knows is Sammy, and he's not telling me anything.

Gary had a similar experience.

WAS THAT A GHOST?

I'm pretty sure cats can see things we can't. Here's my experience. One night the lights in the living room flickered on and off and Speck freaked out. You've never seen a cat jump so high. Then she started to stare at this spot on the ceiling and meow. She only meows when she wants food or when I step on her by accident. She kept hissing at the ceiling. I couldn't see anything.

There was also this one time when I was sleeping in bed. I wasn't quite asleep yet but I was nearly there. It was around one in the morning and everyone else in the house was fast asleep by then. My mother is always the last to go to bed but she never stays up later than midnight and when she goes to bed she checks all the doors and windows are locked and the TV is off and thermostat low and so on.

Well, I started to hear this footstep kind of noise in the hallway. Our house is old and it does creak and groan, but this definitely sounded different to the noises I had heard before. At first I thought it was Dad or my sister making a trip to the bathroom but the footsteps kept on going as if someone was walking backwards and forwards. It sure got Speck going. She jumped out of my bed and started wagging her tailing and stood by my bedroom door taking at good long look at whatever it was that she was staring at, while hiding. Curious, I crept out of bed to take a look with her. Nothing was there.

Debbie also has something curious to report.

At around 6 p.m. every night my cat will jump up and down in the middle of the room, always in exactly the same place as if he is trying to catch something, but I can't see anything. Sometimes he will get quite hysterical and swipe his claws through the air in an attempt to defend himself. Yet, the threat he has perceived is non-existent.
This has gone on for several months now, so I can't explain it away as patterns of light because they would shift. It's really spooky. Just what would make a cat become frightened to the point of engaging in self-defence, other than the ghost of a person or animal?

For Donna, it's clear that her cat has friends in high places.

My cat Jessie has always been very talkative. Sometimes she will talk at a corner of the room. I don't know what she is looking at or talking to and I can't distract her attention. Other times she will follow something coming down the stairs with her eyes and then get up, run to the bottom of the stairs and purr very loudly. She only purrs when she is being cuddled or fed so what was making her behave like this? Could she be seeing ghosts? From time to time she'll also start playing around on the floor as if someone had invisible ribbon and was swirling it around for her to chase. It's like she has an invisible playmate or, as I like to think of it, friends in high places.

Sally doesn't need any convincing that cats can see things we can't.

I've got two cats and they both do this a lot. Suddenly they will crouch down like they are stalking something and walk slowly forward all the time staring at this moving spot. They will do this stalking routine right across the room and then stop when they come to a wall. Then they will walk backwards and forwards beside the wall before eventually curling up close by. Even then they will keep looking back at the wall as if whatever they saw went right through it. Their behaviour is so consistent and so hard to explain I'm convinced they are seeing ghosts or ghost lights.

Elaine has this strange tale to share.

This story isn't about my cat but about my brother's cat. My brother is called Sam and his cat is called Philip—strange and wrong-sounding name for a cat, I know. The point is my brother is a psychologist. He's very rational and not the kind of person with an overactive imagination. Sam told me that for several years before Dad died Philip would come and visit my brother at his office and always sit in the same chair. Sometimes he would doze off to sleep there while my brother worked on his research paper. Each time Dad fell asleep, Philip would jump up and settle down on his lap and doze off too, sometimes the two of them would be snoring together!

Dad always wanted to be buried beside Mum—she died years before him—and threatened to haunt me and Sam if we didn't make sure that happened. When Dad died Sam told me that between his death and the funeral Philip didn't want to go anywhere near Dad's favourite chair. His hair would stand on end. Then as soon as the funeral was over, and we had buried

Dad where he wanted to be buried, Philip jumped on the chair, curled up and went to sleep.

Is it possible that the spirit of Elaine and Sam's father couldn't rest until he had been buried with his beloved wife? Philip is perhaps the only one who can answer that question, and he's not talking.

Andy emailed me with this story about his cat Vlad.

This happens at least twice a week, usually close to midnight. My cat Vlad will run around and around the living room and then go into the hall and sit beside the entrance to my cloakroom. I'll open the door to the cloakroom but he never wants to go inside. He just wants to sit outside it and make a lot of noise. Sometimes he will try and jump up the cloakroom door to get whatever it is he is seeing. He will sit in front of the door and stare at the same spot and jump again. He'll also dart up and down the stairs for no reason or puff himself up into a huge ball of fluff and hiss at nothing.

Andy asked me if I knew whether other people had this kind of experience. I wrote back to tell him that he most certainly was not alone. I believe almost every cat owner could tell a story about their cat having its hair stand up while hissing and spitting at seemingly thin air or their cat darting up the stairs for no reason. In fact, I've heard and read so many stories I could write a whole book devoted to the subject of cats and ghosts. I didn't attach that much significance to my first cat Crystal behaving in this way, but now, as I recognize the same kind of strange behaviour from Merlin and Max I'm absolutely convinced that they *are* seeing something paranormal. I have often seen Merlin in particular all of a sudden look at a spot on the ceiling and then focus furiously on something apparently moving. Only yesterday I found him on top of our piano, trying to scale the wall to get a better look at the ceiling. I looked up and there was no dust there, no insects, no specks of light. Merlin's not as adventurous as Max so this was a very strange place to find him doing his staring routine.

There will always be those who say a cat is seeing a speck of dust, a reflection or an insect, but when these causes have been eliminated, the only explanation I can come up with is that they are chasing spirits. Of course, communication barriers mean that we shall never know for sure, but some of the stories sent to me do seem to indicate that cats are very perceptive of both the physical and spiritual realms and have better connections to the paranormal than we do. In the days of ancient Egypt cats were thought to be divine animals, which is why they were often mummified. It's possible that the Egyptians understood the unique perception of the spirit world that cats have. For the Egyptians cats provided an earthly glimpse of the unseen realm.

Strange footprints in the night

There are many accounts of cats seeing ghosts—and the stories you've read so far are just a few of the many I have heard and read over the years—but there are also an equally high number of stories about cats who appear to visit their owners after the death of their physical bodies. Having researched both human and animal ghosts, I have no hesitation in stating that the ghosts of animals are just as common as those of humans. I've read hundreds of reports of people who have smelled, sensed, heard or felt the spirits of their recently departed pets.

Some people report repeated visits from their pets in spirit but most of the encounters tend to happen only once, as if the cat has returned to say one last goodbye. All the people I spoke to who had experienced this phenomenon told me that the meeting, however brief, gave them great comfort, helped them overcome feelings of guilt and allowed them to move forward with their lives.

Sceptics will put down the experience of a pet visitation as wishful thinking, but if this was the case wouldn't everyone who loved and lost a pet and dearly wanted to see it again be reporting that their cat had returned from the grave to visit them? Some of the people who wrote told me that they had loved many cats over the years, but none of the others had returned, even though they dearly wished they would. Sometimes it is the cat that the owner feels least bonded to that returns and in other cases there are reports of cats returning to visit people who have absolutely no connection to them or indeed belief in the paranormal prior to the visitation. How, for example, can the following stories be explained away?

The first was sent to me by Sonia.

MEOW

Five years ago I moved into a new house. I've never really been much of a cat person but as soon as I moved in this stray cat started visiting me. Before long he was visiting me every day and sometimes more than once a day. I felt sorry for him because he looked battle-scarred and thin, and like me I think he was lonely. I started to look forward to his visits in the evening. After a few months this cat virtually lived in my house and I was shopping for cat

215

food on a weekly basis. He was extremely nervous and I could never pick him up but in time he let me stroke him and he would brush himself against my legs. He had this wonderfully strange meow. It sounded like 'me-now'.

One morning he didn't come for his morning feed. I thought nothing of it but when he didn't appear for the next few days I started to get worried. I really missed him. On the fourth morning I got up and eagerly looked out of the window calling his name. I'd named him Meow. Then I felt a rush of joy as I heard him answer back with his distinctive me-now. I ran outside but couldn't see him. Then I ran in again because it sounded like the sound was coming from inside my house. Then I heard him purring. I spent a few moments trying to find him but I was running late for work so I filled his food bowl and left.

As I walked down the drive my neighbour came rushing up to me with what looked like tears in her eyes. She told me that Meow had been killed by her car last night. She had been driving home and accidentally hit him. She had wanted to tell me last night but it was very late and she had decided to wait until morning. Respectfully, she had wrapped his body in a sheet and placed it in my garden. I didn't know what to say. I couldn't be angry with my neighbour. She was a kind woman and I knew it wasn't her fault.

Later it hit me like a heartbeat. Meow was killed last night but he came to visit me one last time. He knew that I was the only one who would recognize his meow.

Jessie also describes herself as 'not really a cat person'.

WATCHING OVER ME

I'm not really a cat person. I think they are beautiful, but given a choice and if I had the time, space and money I would probably own a dog instead of a cat. That's why I find it so hard to explain something that is happening to me. I've been waking up in the morning with this feeling that a cat is roaming in my bedroom. The sensation is really clear and definite. When I was growing up we owned a cat, and it sounds just like the pitter-patter of a domestic cat walking around, looking for somewhere to lie down. Eventually it will find a place to settle and the footsteps stop. If I get up to take a look there is nothing in the room and the footsteps stop. They don't frighten me. I'm just curious to know what is going on. My boyfriend has checked the loft and house for rats or birds but nothing has been found. The funny thing is I actually find the footsteps reassuring. They only happen when my boyfriend is away on business and I spend the night alone. Do you think a spirit cat is watching over me?

Sandy not only feels blessed by a visit from her departed cat, she also has a strong sense that her cat is looking out for her.

ANGEL WITH WHISKERS

I'm absolutely convinced that my departed cat is my guardian angel. I got him when he was only a few weeks old. I felt so sorry for him because his mother, a stray, had died and he was the only surviving kitten from the litter. He seemed really pathetic and lonely and my heart melted. He shared my bed every night from the first night he arrived. He became my favourite cat of all time—he was black all over except for the tip of his tale which was white. I called him Oliver because somehow he reminded me of the novel. I felt so protective of him, that's why I think he is protecting me now.

Oliver didn't have a very long life—he died suddenly when he was nine—but he packed a lot of fun, cuddles and activity into the time alotted to him. He was my best friend and helped me through school, through retaking my exams and through my first big disappointment in love. Without him I don't know what I would have done. His purrs and his love made everything—even heartache—easier to cope with.

About three months after his passing I started to see cats that looked exactly like him—black all over with a white tip on the tail. I can't explain why but every time I had these sightings I felt comforted and not so alone, as if Oliver was still watching over me and protecting me. Then I began to realize that every time I had a sighting things got better in my life. One time I saw a cat looking exactly like Oliver outside a house that I'd been invited to for a party. When I was inside I met this amazing guy—we're three years happily married now. Another time I applied for an amazing job and the day before I heard that I'd got the job I saw a cat like Oliver again, this time on the television.

Six months ago I saw a cat like Oliver cross the road near where I live. I got really excited because I knew something good was going to happen to me. Sure enough a week later I found out I was pregnant with my first child.

Some people may say that Sandy's story doesn't really count as a spirit cat story because what she sees are living cats that look like Oliver, but the loving and positive feelings she had about Oliver when he was alive are continuing to work miracles now that he has gone.

Megan is convinced a spirit cat is watching over her, but unlike Sandy she has no idea who this cat might be.

BRUSH WITH DEATH

I was driving home one night. I'd been working late and I was rushing to get back in time to put my children to bed. I was worried I wouldn't make it as it was getting close to their bedtime. Well, it was getting dark and this cat suddenly darted into the road in front of me. There was no time to brake and I felt sick to my stomach when I heard my car hit it. I hated myself for what I had done. I looked in my rear-view mirror and saw the cat's body lying in the road. I wondered if there was any chance I could save it so I parked my car on the side of the road. Just as I was getting out a car whizzed past me driving on the wrong side of the road—the side of the road I would have been driving on if I had not pulled my car over.

I started to shake all over. It really hit me. I had been seconds from death and this cat had saved my life. I looked in the road for the cat I had hit but there was nothing there, absolutely nothing. I had clearly seen the cat lying on the road in my rear-view mirror and it had been absolutely still. I know cats are fast but there is no way that it could have moved away in such a short space of time, especially after being hit hard by a car. I've never owned a cat, never thought about owning one, but I am one hundred per cent convinced that for some unknown reason a spirit cat chose to save my life and for that I will be forever grateful.

Ron's story is similar in that he also feels that a spirit cat saved his life.

My wife died last year and it was a very lonely time. My cat Bambi was a huge comfort because she was always there when it got too much. Bambi died three months ago, and although I have met someone wonderful I still miss her deeply. The house seems lonely without her.

One night I woke up with a splitting headache. I also felt a familiar padding on my legs and heard Bambi meowing. It was the same kind of meow she used to make when she wanted me to feed her—fast. I thought I must be dreaming but I couldn't settle because my head hurt. I dragged myself out of bed and went to the kitchen to get some water and some painkillers.

When I got to the kitchen I noticed to my horror that I had forgotten to turn my gas oven off. Gas fumes were pouring out. I switched the oven off, opened as many windows as I could and stood for a long while in the fresh air. As I did I felt Bambi weaving in and out of my legs and I knew in that moment that Bambi had used one of her nine lives to save me.

Ron's experience is remarkable, and it is also incredibly rare. In the great majority of cases cats don't return from the grave to save their owner's lives; they return briefly to say goodbye and give their owners much-needed comfort. This can reassure someone that it is not only the spirit of their cat that lives on after death, but their own spirit as well. The experience is also hugely comforting for owners wondering if they could have prevented their cat's death and harbouring guilt (If only I hadn't let him out that day or warned him better to stay away from roads . . .) as well as those owners never given the chance to say goodbye because their cat died unexpectedly, whether from accident or sudden illness.

Like human ghosts, sightings of cat ghosts seem to offer reassurance and comfort. Sue's daughter Sally had this experience after the death of her twenty-year-old cat Pop.

My son Simon struggled with poor health for much of his childhood. When he was eleven he was bedridden for almost a year because of a back problem. He's in his twenties now and is laid low with arthritis again. Recently, he's been telling me that he feels something at the bottom of his bed, to the left of his feet. I knew exactly what he was talking about. I told him it was Pop. I reminded him that when he spent that year in bed when he was eleven Pop had slept there every day and it was very comforting. Pop died five or so years ago but my son and I truly believe that she is still bringing comfort to us.

Cat ghosts can also appear to let worried owners know that they are doing just fine in the spirit world. This is the feeling Jill got when she had no choice but to have her cat Claws put down.

DOING JUST FINE

I've owned many wonderful cats over the last forty-five years. Several of them have had to be put down and on each occasion I found myself second-guessing the decision. Could I have done more? Did I do the right thing? Did I miss anything? Then something extrordinary happened last year and it really put my mind at rest.

My twenty-year-old gal Claws was put down. She had kidney failure and a tumour, there was a considerable amount of water in her stomach and she could barely walk. Deep down I knew it was the right decision but always at the back of my mind I wondered if I should have pressed for more tests.

When the vet gave Claws her first shot I held her in my arms. I told her how much I loved her and how much I didn't want her to suffer any more. I wrapped her in a blanket to make sure she was cosy and rocked her back and forwards like a baby. The eye contact between us never broke until hers eventually closed. The vet gave her another shot and then asked me if he could check for a heartbeat. He didn't need to because I knew Claws had left me.

I loved Claws passionately. I don't mind admitting to you that she was like a child to me. For about a month or two after I felt very low. Then one night while I was lying in bed thinking about her I felt the thump of a cat landing on the side of my bed and a familiar chirping sound. It sounded exactly like the thump and chirp Claws used to make when she settled down to sleep with me at night. I thought it might be Blue, my other cat, but Blue prefers to sleep in the kitchen. This happened for five nights in a row, so I knew I wasn't dreaming it. The thud on the bed felt real as did the chirp. There was nothing there and I know it was Claws's way of reassuring me that she was fine and that I shouldn't feel guilty any more because everything was all right. Also, for a few weeks after her death, my bedroom door started to open as if Claws was opening it with her paw, which made me feel that her spirit was with me.

Please share this story with as many people as you can as I know lots of us worry when we have to make painful decisions if we have made the right one. I think that if every decision we make for our cats is made out of love then our cat can never resent us, in this life or the next.

Cats and the afterlife

Love, whether in human or animal form, can cross the boundaries of time and space, and many people who have lost beloved pets truly believe that their animals continue to visit them in spirit. After my first cat Crystal died I would often sense her presence or feel the brush of her body against my legs. I was never frightened by these experiences—quite the contrary: they seemed the most comforting and natural thing in the world. And the more stories I hear from people who have had similar experiences the more convinced I am that contact with a beloved deceased cat is possible. For me and others it's clear that distance and even death cannot break the psychic bond between human and cat.

At first when I made a point of collecting such stories I thought many of them would be unsettling, like the story of the haunted Fairport Harbor Lighthouse in northern Ohio, where a number of witnesses allegedly saw the ghost of a cat, described as a gray puff of smoke. Many years later, the mummified remains of a cat were found in a wall during some repair work. Did they find the body of the ghostly feline? I had planned a chapter in this book devoted to this kind of spooky encounter, but I soon discovered that scary tales about deceased pets are incredibly rare. Most cat owners feel only relief, comfort, joy and a sense of closure after a visit from a deceased cat. A visit from a dead relative or loved one might well cause panic but when the visit is from a beloved cat they usually feel blessed. It's not surprising really because spirit cats are the same loving friends you had when they were alive.

As I was writing this chapter I got an email from Jenny, and given the great timing and relevance of her story, just had to include it here.

Todd our black and white cat was with us for quite a few years when I was a child. I'm convinced he was very young when we got him. He liked sleeping in the airing cupboard if the door was left open. He would put his paw in and squeeze his head through until he eventually got in, but I think his favourite place was on my bed.

I can remember curling up in bed on many occasions with a good book. Todd would jump up, circle round clockwise and anticlockwise a few times, and curl up in a small dip between my bottom and the calves of my legs to get comfortable then nod off to sleep. It felt so nice hearing the purring and slight snore as he slept. His body warmth was like a lukewarm hot-water bottle.

I can't remember how old I was when Todd died. To be honest, I think our grumpy neighbour Mr Smith killed him, but of course I have no proof. Mr Smith didn't like children and I don't think he liked cats either. My mum told me that Mr Smith found Todd in his greenhouse dead. There is no way Todd would have gone in there, because it would have been far too hot.

I missed Todd badly, but not long after he died I do remember a particular night when I went up to bed. Lying there with my book in one hand and my other hand propping up my chin, to my amazement I felt something jump on my bed. Looking over my left shoulder I saw a visible dip from the back of my bottom to the calves of my legs and felt that same warmth that I felt before. My heart started racing and I dropped my book on the floor. I was definitely not dreaming, Todd had come back for one last doze with me.

All these years later Jenny has never forgotten that experience and the confirmation it gave that her beloved cat was still with her. Angel also believes her cat came back for one last goodbye.

BURNING BRIGHT

Tiger was my baby. She was most the most stunningly beautiful Persian-cross you can imagine. She also had the loudest purr you could imagine—now I know why they call them purrsians. I lived with Tiger and loved her every second of the five years we spent together, but she got very ill and needed to be put to sleep.

One morning I was sitting drinking my tea and watching breakfast TV when I felt something jump on the back of the sofa and brush past my neck. Then I felt something kneading my left shoulder. Tiger always used to do that when she was alive. It was part of our morning ritual. I also felt warmth, happiness and light all around me. I wasn't daydreaming or dreaming. I didn't imagine it. Tiger came back for one last goodbye.

Angel also sent me a few lines from a poem by author Linda Barnes, which I'd like to include here because it complements this chapter's theme so well.

> They will not go quietly,
> the cats who' ve shared our lives.
> In subtle ways they let us know
> their spirit still survives.

Speaking from personal experience, one of the most heart-warming things about a visitation from a spirit cat is the promise that this isn't really goodbye at all and one day there will be a reunion in the afterlife, as described so fondly in the well-known story of the Rainbow Bridge—a mythical place inspired by a poem first published in the 1980s. In this poem, whose original author is uncertain, the spirit or soul of a beloved pet departs to a sunny meadow, where it plays happily until reunited with its owner in death.

When the owner's death is close the pet senses this and before owner and pet go to heaven together there is an emotional meeting between the two.

They may not be angels in the traditional sense, but with their empathy, patience, devotion and unconditional love, cats sound a lot like angels to me. Like angels, they simply love us and watch over us in this life and the next.

Andy certainly believes that his beloved cat Poe hasn't said goodbye and never will. Here is his very special story. I know it's special because when I was adding it to this book Merlin jumped up for the first time on my keyboard.

PASSING THROUGH

It was asking for trouble naming a black cat Poe. But unlike the eponymous feline in Edgar Allan Poe's chilling tale 'The Black Cat' , my Poe returned to comfort and inspire me.

Far from being gloomy and moody, he was my little ray of sunshine. A friendlier, more agreeable cat I have yet to meet. Fuelled by an energy and a lust for life that were exhausting just to watch, my woodland warrior was kindness itself. Unless you happened to be a bird or small mammal, that is! For Poe quickly became an expert hunter.

I only had fifteen short months with him. One summer and one Christmas to share and treasure, that was all. He died in my arms after being hit by a car. And how quickly it was over. In despair, I watched the light go out of his eyes. My Poe was gone.

Or so I thought. Life may have been finished with Poe, but Poe was not finished with life! I cried day and night. I could hardly speak, words sticking in my throat as I choked on grief. And then something wonderful and totally unexpected happened. My Poe came back to me in spirit form. I was sitting in my conservatory, totally consumed by grief, when the room suddenly filled with Poe's presence. It was just as though he had walked into the room. It was so strong that I reached down, half—expecting to touch fur. At once I felt cheered and heartened. I hadn't been looking for this, hadn't willed it to happen. Poe himself chose his moment to come back to me, to ease my devastation. I should have known that such a loving cat would not just leave me grieving.

Something told me to go out into the garden. As I did so, I was almost knocked off my feet by the strength of Poe's presence. I quickly realized that my little angel had become part of nature. He was now in everything around me. He was in the grass, the flowers, the sun, the rain, the wind that shook the barley and the whispering trees. I knew in that instant that whenever I wanted to feel close to Poe, all I had to do was go to some natural place and there he' d be.

I'd always kept an open mind about paranormal phenomena. I'd retained an interest and had always acknowledged that inexplicable things happen to ordinary people, but what was behind it all, I'd never been sure. The events of the months following the loss of dear Poe convinced me beyond doubt that that there is life after death and that the spirits of our lost loved ones regularly visit us, no question about that.

Throughout the magical summer, autumn and winter of 2008/9, Poe continually showed himself with such strength and frequency as to be undeniable. There wasn't one massive, irrefutable piece of proof. It was a series of smaller events, coincidences and synchronicities that went way, way beyond chance. Many, many times it has been a tangible feeling of Poe still being around that has to me been the most convincing. I can't show that to anyone, can't prove it to disbelievers. It is something very personal that passes between me and Poe that people will choose to believe or they won't. After that first, crucial breakthrough, I certainly didn't need any convincing!

Theresa, I began reading one of your Angel books. I had reached the chapter that explained how our lost loved ones often show themselves by the appearance of a white feather. I was reading this chapter when I got a sudden urge to look up. As I did so, I saw a small white feather, distant, airborne, floating down out of the clear, blue sky. As I watched in amazement, the feather homed in and landed right at my feet.

This was the first of many instances of white feathers appearing unexpectedly in prominent places at times of doubt and questioning. They were always accompanied by a potent air that told me that my treasured feline was at my side.

One day, leaf fragments formed the distinct shape of a cat on my window. It was so clear and spontaneous that I took a picture of it. When developed, many orbs were visible around the cat shape. This was the only time I have ever captured orbs on film.

This shape appeared on the day that I left my mundane, soul-destroying job and stayed there, through strong winds and heavy rain, until the day I began my dream animal-care job, on which it vanished, despite the day being calm and still.

One summer afternoon I planted some bluebell bulbs around Poe's memorial tree. A couple of days later I heard that the plaque was in place on the cat pen that I had sponsored in his memory at a local rescue centre. I drove over to see it (down Bluebell Way!) and was stunned to see Poe's absolute double, the first cat in his sponsored pen. And bearing in mind what I'd just planted for him, the breath caught in my throat as I saw that the little black cat's name was Bluebell!

Poe would often come in during the night and sneak upstairs like a naughty schoolboy, past his curfew. He would curl up and go to sleep in the washbasket in the bedroom. Six months to the day since I lost him, at exactly the time that I had to let him go, I heard a distinct creak from the washbasket. Turning on the bedside lamp, I saw my cat Parsley staring wide-eyed at the basket. She had heard it too.

I have never actually seen Poe's ghost directly and firmly. Many times I see a movement out of the corner of my eye— something small and black—but when I look round, I see nothing. These fleeting glimpses are always accompanied by those very strong feelings that I'm the company of my precious puss. It's nothing more

234

scientific than that—a feeling—but when it comes, it is unmistakable.

One of the most striking events happened one evening as I was emailing an animal psychic who had visited my house and successfully contacted Poe's spirit. (That's another story too long to include here!) I was updating her on things that she'd said that had proved to be true when one of my cats, Jewel, began staring intently at the foot of the stairs—exactly the place that the psychic had said that Poe was while she was in touch with him. Jewel was quickly joined by another of my cats, Pepsi. The intrepid pair stalked over to that spot, every strand of fur on the highest alert. They stared unflinchingly at the foot of the stairs. In unison, both began to mew plaintively. I moved over beside them, and there it was, that powerful, true sense of Poe's presence, but even more compelling this time.

The world stopped turning. A silence descended that was thick and complete. No birds. No cars. Just an absolute silence, as rare as it was chilling. I traced Poe's path as he moved up the stairs, turned then descended. A stair creaked. Then the one below it. Still my cats stared. I became frightened, because I was clearly in the midst of something very weird and I didn't know how to handle it. As fear swept through me, the spell was broken and the world returned to normal. Birds resumed their singing. Car engines once again droned. Pepsi and Jewel wandered off.

I so wish I hadn't lost my nerve that day because he hasn't come through as strongly as that again. I'm disappointed in myself for blocking Poe's attempt to take things to another level only because I wasn't ready for it.

During those devastating days following the loss of sweet Poe, I reassessed my life. I vowed to Poe that I would dedicate the rest of my life to animal care, in his memory. He communicated back that he would help me do this. And so he did. There followed a series of inexplicable coincidences that led me to leave my long-term civil service job and get my dream position as an animal care assistant at Easterleigh Animal Sanctuary in Lytham St Annes. The way events unfolded and fell neatly into place for me would be dismissed as being too far-fetched if they were the plot of a film or book. I don't pretend to understand how, but I remain convinced that Poe engineered these synchronicities to allow me to look after animals, every day, in his name. That's a truly wonderful thing.

One of the things that the animal psychic picked up on was the fact that I had my eye on a cat in desperate need of a good home, but I was worried that Poe might think I was trying to replace him (How could she possibly know that?), which was precisely what I was feeling. She told me that Poe was urging me to get the cat and love her in his memory. He didn't mind at all. I did get the kitten and I named her Bluebell in tribute to that first cat housed in Poe's memorial rescue pen.

Poe's approval of my rescuing Bluebell was evidenced the first time she was allowed to go outside. You might think that using a cat flap comes naturally to a cat. Oh no, no, no. I toiled for five days to try to get Bluebell to master it, but she just didn't get it. I tried everything, including getting down on my hands and knees and pushing the flap with my head. Not a flicker from Bluey. After five long, long days of trying, I said out loud, 'Poe, if you're here, can you show her what to do?' I looked on in astonishment as Bluebell cocked her head to one side, listened hard, then passed confidently straight through the catflap. I was delighted because this was firm evidence that Poe was watching over Bluebell, as well as me.

This was further displayed when I was at work one day and got a sudden, overwhelming feeling that I had to go home. This had never happened before and was so potent that I could not ignore it. I raced home to find a stricken Bluebell, flat out and desperately ill. I rushed her to the vet's, where she got the immediate treatment required to help her recover from a dangerously high temperature. I am convinced that my sudden need to rush home that day was Poe telling me that Bluebell needed me urgently.

There was another time when my tomcat Pepsi hadn't shown his furry face for over eighteen hours. He normally enjoys an outdoor life but hadn't been out of sight for that length of time before. After an extended period of extreme worry, I asked Poe to find Pepsi and send him home. Within a few short minutes, Pepsi appeared.

Are all these things just coincidence? Can chance and probability stretch that far, time and time again? I believe not. I remain totally convinced that Poe is watching over not just me, but my cats as well, guiding us and keeping us safe. I would never ask him to appear, just to prove the point. I just know that he's always there when I need him, truly the angel on my shoulder.

Time moves on and pain eases, although I'll miss him for ever. Sadly, I don't feel Poe as strongly or as often now. I've heard it said that at times of emotional crisis our psychic powers are greatly enhanced. That could explain why we pick up on the spirit of our departed loved ones only sometimes. It's not that they're not there for us all the time—they are—it's us that can only connect with them when emotionally charged.

The song 'Northern Skies' [the uncredited extra track at the end of the *These Streets* album by Scottish crooner Paolo Nutini] is one that I turn to time and time again when remembering my Poe. Referring as it does to the great sense of passing through, I realize that Poe was doing exactly that. His time on earth, woefully brief, was just a stepping stone for him. He exists in another form, in another world, that is just as real as this one. When he thinks I need him, he calls in to comfort and reassure me. I'm privileged to have known him while he was here and I'll love him all my life.

There's an old Tibetan proverb that says, 'It's better to live for twenty-five days as a tiger than for a thousand years as a sheep.' That nicely sums up my Poe and the way he chose to live his short, happy life. If I had our time over again, would I have kept him in to keep him safe? Absolutely not. Poe was and remains a free spirit. He wouldn't have been happy any other way.

Thank you, Andy and Poe, from the bottom of my heart, as I know this story will resonate with people who have loved and lost their precious cats everywhere!

Now that you've gone

The loss of a beloved cat can be as devastating to some as the loss of a child. Cats are family. They offer companionship, empathy, love, play and fun as well as opportunities to nurture. It's no surprise then that the death of a cat can result in great grief, a grief deepened by the fact that there is no socially accepted way to mourn, for example with a funeral or memorial service. As a result many cat owners feel isolated and alone in their loss. There is also a sense of emptiness, a hole inside that used to be filled with love, play and laughter. It doesn't help when you can hear friends and colleagues thinking, even if they aren't saying, What's the big deal? It's only a cat. Move on.

When Crystal died I cried for days, weeks, and just at the moment I thought I was feeling better something would remind me of her—another cat, a whisker on the floor, her food bowl—and I'd cry all over again. Then a month or so later I finally accepted the loss and decided to move on. Crystal was irreplaceable and I was never going to risk my heart being torn apart again. I was never going to own another cat.

Looking back, I think I made things much harder for myself after Crystal died than they need have been. Crying it out was positive because holding back the emotion would have meant that the tears might come to the surface again at unexpected times. Crying with my mum, who loved Crystal too, and talking to her about my feelings of loss was also positive because she was the one person who understood so I didn't feel completely isolated. What wasn't so positive was that I didn't create some kind of memorial, such as a memory box with a swatch of fur or a paw print, or ritual of remembrance. We couldn't afford a proper funeral, and twenty-five years ago the importance of funerals for beloved pets just wasn't as commonly recognized as it is today.

To ease my pain my mum took care of Crystal's remains. To this day I don't know what happened to them. My mum died a few years later and it was something I never discussed with her. The only things I have left are a few faded photographs, which in my grief I nearly threw away. I'm glad I didn't in the end because they provide me with a positive and lasting focal point of remembrance—something I urge all pet owners to create for themselves when their pet dies.

There is no need to feel pressured to let go of the memories you have of your deceased cat. In fact, psychologists believe that retaining a bond with a lost loved one is a healthy part of grieving and recovery. So if you are mourning the loss of a cat talk about the times you shared, remember the special relationship you shared, treasure photographs, write a book or a poem or make a memory box. This continuing bond will not—as I wrongly thought—prevent the possibility of bonding with a new cat when the time feels right.

Hopefully, the stories, words and thoughts in this chapter will have shown you that when your beloved cat eventually dies, although you can't physically touch them any more the bond between you and your cat has not been broken. You will simply experience them in a different way. Your cat will stay alive in your heart, and in spirit form can even be with you more intensely than before.

Finally, perhaps the biggest mistake I made when Crystal died was making the 'never replace her/him' resolve. For close to twenty-five years I hardened my heart. I told myself that there could never be another cat like Crystal and I couldn't bear the pain of loving and losing a cat again.

But two little kittens changed all that, and I now know that although it is true that you can never replace a cat, you can fill that emptiness in your home and in your heart. Maureen believes this is exactly what her departed cat wanted her to do.

LILY

Lily died at 2 pm on a sunny Monday afternoon in April. I was with her at the vet's when she died in my arms. I'd known for weeks that she would have to be put down but even so when the inevitable happened I wasn't prepared at all for the hurt and grief I would feel.

My only small comfort was that she hadn't suffered too much. She had probably thought she was just drifting off to sleep. She didn't know that she would never wake up. Tears rolling down my cheeks, I carried her home that day with her special pink blanket and buried her in my back garden with her favourite toys.

I'd had the privilege to share my life with Lily for twenty-two years, and every moment—except when she vanished once for a week and I was sick with worry—had been a joy. I'd had her so long I found it hard to imagine what life would be like without her. I didn't realize how much of my day was structured around her from getting up in the morning to feeding her to sitting watching television in the evening with her purring on my lap. I loved that cat, and now I would be without her and alone.

The day after I'd buried Lily I started to sense her around me. My friends told me I was being daft and I thought they were right. They told me it was best if I threw out all of Lily's things so I wasn't constantly reminded. I tried to throw them out but couldn't. My brother told me to get another cat but I thought this would be like a betrayal of Lily and point-blank refused because no cat could replace my Lily. When I woke up in the morning I could hear her purring and in the evening I felt her jump on my bed. I felt her sitting on her favourite windowsill. When I walked around the house I could feel Lily brush against my leg. She was everywhere I was.

This went on for about two months. Then this stray cat turned up at my door. He was a rough and ready black and greyish-white tom and so different from my delicate Lily, a silver-shaded British short hair with impeccable manners. I tried to chase him away but he was persistent and one evening when I was putting out the rubbish he shot inside. I dropped my rubbish bag and followed him in. He ran into my living room and I could tell right away that he was aware of Lily's presence because he just stared at the windowsill she used to sit on with his tail all puffed up. Fascinated, I waited to see what would happen. I watched the stray stare at the window ledge for at least five minutes. Then in a flash he stopped staring, trotted over and jumped onto the ledge, licked his hind legs, curled up and went to sleep. I didn't have the heart to push the cat out so I let him sleep. Then when he woke up a few hours later he gobbled up some of Lily's gourmet food that I still had lurking in my cupboard.

That night when I sat down in front of the television I didn't feel Lily around me as I had done before. I just had this overwhelming sense that she had now gone over to the other side and that letting another cat sleep where she had always loved hanging out was her way of telling me that she wanted me to be happy, because she was happy in spirit.

The stray moved in with me and he is such a character. It took him just a week or so to feel really at home and now—just as Lily did—he has taken ownership of me and my house. I don't mind in the slightest. Nothing will ever replace Lily but the stray—I've called him Larry—has helped me feel so much better about her death. I think she sent Larry my way because she wanted me to be happy again.

Think about it.

Like Maureen, many cat lovers are convinced that a spirit cat often plays a large role in sending a new kitten or cat to them. Some have told me that when they least expected it a cat somehow turned up and enriched their lives in ways they could not have imagined. This is exactly how it felt for me when I adopted Max and Merlin. It felt as if Crystal was somehow looking on and purring.

It isn't a betrayal to open your heart to another cat. Naturally, you will miss your old pet deeply, and no cat will be the same as your lost love, but it would be an insult to their memory if you never took the plunge again. If you've had a fantastic relationship with a cat you can repeat it with another. It is the relationship between human and cat, not the cat, you are replacing.

Owning or saving the life of another cat is a way of keeping your departed cat's memory alive every day. What finer memorial could there be to the cat you have lost than rehoming a kitten from a shelter or cattery? I've had Max and Merlin for close to six months now and not a day goes by that I don't thank Crystal for sending them to me. So, if your beloved cat dies and you find yourself making the 'never replace' statement, you might just want to think again!

8. More Than Just a Cat

Time spent with cats is never wasted.
Sigmund Freud

Why do people love cats? Let me count the ways

Cats have this way of silently padding into our hearts, bringing with them their grace, mystery, independence, love and innate telepathy, all of which can soothe the energy of those around them. They comfort us with their purring and cuddling, and the way they rub their faces on our hands or legs brings a sense of warmth, but their quirkiness, playful wit and unpredictability can also keep us on our toes. They are fiercely intelligent and intuitive and have this amazing ability to communicate with us without words. Ever noticed your cat staring at her food bowl and back at you, reminding you gently but assertively that it is time to be fed?

Whether it is a cat's independent but affectionate nature, mysterious beauty or simply the deep and healing bond that it can form with a human, there is much to adore. The soft fur, the comforting purring, the grace, the wild and playful spirit and the sense of connection and understanding are some of the

247

lasting and lingering impressions formed after spending time with a cat, but none of these can really answer the question, Why do people love cats? Perhaps the answer cannot actually be written down; it can only be *felt* when you have spent time around a cat.

Many cat owners I have spoken to over the years and while writing this book have told me that their cat is more than just a pet to them. The bond formed between owner and cat is a lifelong one that involves empathy, companionship, unconditional love and, as many of the stories in this book have demonstrated, telepathy. And this cat–human bond not only has the power to heal and in some instances save lives, it can also change us in ways we don't realize. If we allow cats to work their magic on us, they can make us better people.

Ron got in touch a few years ago to send me this story told to him by a friend. It reads very much like a parable of unconditional love and I don't know who actually wrote it, but I've never forgotten it because it is so moving and powerful. I hope it will linger long in your mind and your heart too.

UGLY

When I was a kid I grew up in a really tough area. I was a tough kid myself. I had to be. Otherwise I wouldn't have survived.

About the age of ten I got friendly with this group of boys. We called ourselves the Clan. Desperate to fit in, I went along with everything they said and did. I bitterly regret that now, but back then I didn't know any better.

We were into petty crime and stuff. Nothing serious but I do remember us breaking windows and stealing things. I also remember us torturing a stray cat. This cat was really ugly. It had no tail and some kind of deformity in its front legs. Life had clearly been so—for this cat. He was skin and bones and there were sores all over his head and neck. When this cat came up to us one night hoping for food one of the kids thought it would be fun to stub a cigarette out on it. Another thought it would be fun to kick it. I was encouraged to throw stones. Mercifully the cat dodged the stones.

I saw this cat again on a number of occasions. Incredibly, he would still come up to us meowing frantically. On one occasion he bumped his head on my legs, hoping for a stroke. But each time he got the same reaction from us, which was to taunt, hit or kick him away. Once I saw him near our flat and my mum threw a bucket of water over him. Our neighbours did the same thing. Nobody wanted such an ugly cat close to them.

One day when I was walking back from school with my bag trailing on the ground I found this ugly cat lying in the street. He was covered in blood. I don't know what had happened to him but it looked like he had been kicked or bitten by some dogs—there were some really vicious ones in our area. Curious, I leaned over. I'd never seen a dead cat before. As I bent over I could hear that he was still gently breathing.

I knelt down close to him and he slowly lifted his head. He looked at me and it was like a bolt of energy shot through me, that's the only way I can describe it. My eyes filled with tears and I gently cradled his head in my hand. In that instant I felt so much love for this cat, it hurt me. I told him I was sorry I had hurt him and that his life had been so bad and so lonely. I asked him to forgive me.

Then as this cat lay dying he did the most incredible thing. He started to lick my hand. He was dying but still longing for love and kindness. I picked him up and held him tight. I could hear the faintest sound of purring.

Time stood still and for an all too brief instant this ugly stray was the most exquisite creature in the world. We stared at each other without blinking and it felt as if our hearts connected. This cat trusted me to be there for him. Then the purring stopped and I knew that his spirit had gone.

By now my mum had come outside looking for me. I didn't hear her shouting at me to drop the dead cat because I had blood all over me and my school stuff. I didn't want to let him go. I turned away and gently put him in some bushes where later that evening I would return and give him a proper burial.

As I walked home with my mum scolding me I thought long and hard about how this ugly stray cat had changed my mind about so many things and taught me more than my parents, my school or books or TV shows probably could about what humility, forgiveness, gratitude, love and compassion mean. This cat had been ugly on the outside but he had been beautiful on the inside. I had been ugly on the inside and it was time to make big changes in my life.

I can honestly say that those precious moments with a dying stray cat changed my life completely. I stopped hanging out with the Clan and got my head down at school and am now training to become a vet. I used to want to be popular, rich and cool, but from that day forwards I have tried to be like an ugly stray cat. I can honestly stay that the best things in my life all came to me after I had opened my heart to an ugly cat no one ever cared for.

Ron's story is intense, but if you've ever lived with cats you're sure to recognize their influence on your life. Like Ron, it wasn't until I welcomed Merlin and Max into my life that I became consciously aware of the subtle and graceful way that cats can teach us powerful lessons about life and love. One of the first lessons the kittens taught me was about caring for sick animals. My efforts to avoid the difficulties of bonding and caring for animals that have been mistreated backfired when Max, a pedigree cat I had purchased, got seriously ill and suffered terribly, putting the whole family through weeks of heartache and anxiety. However, because we have been through hardship together the bond I now have with my cats is much deeper and more rewarding than it might have been, reminding me that, just as in human relationships, we need to care for our pets in both sickness and in health.

Cat wisdom

I've met many thinkers and many cats, but the wisdom of cats is infinitely superior.
Hippolyte Taine

In the six months that they have graced our home, I have learned a lot from my cats. I've learned to take my time, be patient but never lose my focus. If Merlin doesn't get what he wants straight away he will sit quietly and wait for it. In the morning after he has woken me up he will sit by the door staring at me quietly. If I doze off he will jump on my pillow and start cleaning himself, very noisily. Most of the time his gentle persistence does the trick, but if I'm really sleepy he isn't afraid to ask more directly. To get my attention he will climb up the curtains or scratch at my bedclothes, or he will chase a piece of fluff around on the floor. Even if he isn't getting what he wants he still has fun reminding me that life is good and I should enjoy it.

Little Max is teaching me that there should always be time in our day for sitting quietly and relaxing with the ones you love. There can be great peace and clarity in solitude. Every day does not have to be packed with an endless list of 'to dos' . Sometimes we should just unwind, stretch out and watch the clouds roll by. Indeed, both Max and Merlin remind me that even if I'm busy working, writing or doing anything, there can always be time for laughter and affection.

Above all, though, my cats don't just bring love and companionship; they also bring me insight and inspiration, because they see something worth loving and comforting in me that I may not always see in myself. I'm sure many cat owners would agree that perhaps this is the greatest gift that their cats give them. I'm going to bring in Leslie's email here because I think it sums up beautifully what I am trying to say.

HEAVEN SENT

I'm disabled, have been for most of my life. I've also suffered serious bouts of depression. One time when I got low my doctor suggested I go into hospital, but in the end I didn't need to. I stayed at home with my cat Callie, who didn't leave my side except to eat and use her litter tray. She understands both my physical and my emotional pain. She senses when I really need her and when I'm feeling stronger. She is more intuitive than any nurse or doctor could ever be. She just seems to know what I need, whether it's sitting quietly with me when I work on my PC or purring loudly by my side when I need to rest—she just *knows*. Call me daft or crazy, but in my mind I think she is what we humans should try to be. She doesn't judge me; she loves me unconditionally. She is gentle and understanding and forgives me quickly when I'm moody or when I mess up. She always seems to be content, as if she knows some secret about life that I don't. She's my role model. She's heaven sent.

I'm sure that Leslie's words will strike a chord with many cat lovers. Cats don't demand much from us but they give us so much in return. Like angels they love and watch over us in this life, and when the time comes to say goodbye they may very well watch over us in the next. I know that I find the idea of my cats waiting for me in the afterlife incredibly comforting. Indeed, I'm not sure I'd want to be there without Crystal, Merlin and Max. For me, heaven simply wouldn't be heaven without cats.

*   *   *

Now it's your turn!

I hope that reading this book will have convinced you that of all the feline characteristics that have intrigued and delighted people throughout the centuries it is their psychic and spiritual natures that fascinate us the most and draw us closest to cats. If you have any incredible stories about cats—or indeed any hero pet or remarkable animal that has saved, brightened, transformed or inspired your life in any way—I warmly invite you to share them with me. (Details about how to do this can be found at the front of this book.) You never know, they might end up in a future book and inspire others to share their home with a cat. Every cat owner and cat lover has a cat story to tell. Now it's your turn!

Epilogue: Nine Lives?

Where there is great love there are always miracles.
Willa Cathar

Everyone has heard the saying, 'A cat has nine lives.' It's unclear where this myth originates from but it is likely that it is connected with a cat's marvellous ability to fall on its feet when dropping from a height. It may also have something to do with the fact that cats can be great survivors. There are a number of incredible stories about cats cheating death, like that of Sam, the World War II survivor, who cheated death not once but three times.

CLINGING FOR DEAR LIFE

During World War II Sam was a pet of the crew of the German battleship *Bismark*. On 27 May 1941 the ship was sunk by Allied forces with only 115 of the 2,200 men on board surviving. Several hours after the ship capsized British sailors from HMS *Cossack* discovered him clinging for dear life to a board floating on the ocean. They took pity on the cat and adopted him as their mascot.

Sam sailed with the *Cossack* for several months until the ship was damaged by a German torpedo and sank with the loss of 159 dead, but Sam survived again. He was then transferred to an aircraft carrier, HMS *Ark Royal*, which was torpedoed by a German submarine, sinking off the coast of Gibraltar. The ship sank slowly and mercifully all but one member of the crew survived. Once again, Sam was discovered clinging to a plank. Fortunately for Sam, he then got the chance to live out the rest of his life on dry land with a retired seaman in Belfast. He died of natural causes at the age of fourteen.

Another cat with an unlikely but inspiring survival story is Precious, a nine-pound pampered Persian.

PRECIOUS

On 11 September 2001 Precious was alone in the New York apartment of his owners, Steve and D. J. Kerr, which was located directly across the street from the Twin Towers, when the buildings collapsed. Every window in the flat was shattered, spraying glass and metal shrapnel inside and then filling it with a cloud of toxic dust.

Things were set to get much worse for Precious. The apartment building was so badly damaged and dangerous that the Kerrs were not allowed to return to look for their cat. This meant that Precious, an indoor cat, had to fend for herself for eighteen days until an animal rescue team discovered her on the building roof. She was dehydrated, thin and very dirty but otherwise healthy.

Alongside these displays of courage and resilience are the cats who display incredible intelligence or skill. This book just wouldn't be complete without mention of Nora, the piano-playing cat whose musical talents have caught the imagination of over twenty million people on YouTube. And when stories like those of Nora, Sam and Precious are combined with the long-standing belief that cats are psychic or even divine messengers of comfort and healing, it's easy to see how and why the nine lives myth has taken such a firm hold.

Sadly, though, as anyone who has ever said a premature goodbye to a cherished cat companion knows, cats don't have nine lives. They only have one to live, but what many cat owners find so enchanting about their cats is that they live that one life with courage, generosity, resourcefulness, compassion, dignity and a capacity for making the most of each moment. There's much we humans can learn from them.

Coexisting with this myth is the idea that cats are disloyal and will only follow the hand that feeds. This myth just won't go away. Sure, cats are independent but also need love, food, water and a place to sleep, and whoever does this job the best will get their love and loyalty in return. In other words, cats give back as much love as we give them. And the more love we give them the better we feel.

I once heard that cats have nine lives because when they are blessed with loving owners who treat them right they give a few of these lives to their owners in gratitude. I'm inclined to believe this might just have a ring of truth about it. Since Max and Merlin's arrival I really have discovered a whole new zest for life. They surround me with love, especially on those days when I really don't want to face the world. I wake up and see them chasing invisible air balls and feel better right away. They don't just help me get out of bed, they help me get outside myself, and any problems I'm stressing about are released—even if only for a moment.

There's an old saying that until one has loved an animal, a part of one's soul remains untouched. As you've seen in this book, cats are psychic and spiritual creatures, and if we let them they can touch our hearts. They remind us that no matter who we feel love for in this life, human or animal, love is what gives us meaning. The very fact that we can love another being expands who we are and gives us a higher perspective.

I feel truly blessed to be sharing my life with two delightful cats. The love and laughter they bring into my life is a daily reminder of something I—and I'm sure many of us—all too often forget, that miracles are not just possible, but probable. So if you're looking to breathe a little magic, comfort and sweetness into your life, you may want to spend some time with a cat. You see, the miracles you're hoping for might already be before your very eyes, waiting for you to notice and reach out to them.

I'll leave you, for now, with two of my favourite cat quotations.

I love cats because I love my home and after
a while they become its visible soul.
Jean Cocteau

A beating heart and an angel's soul, covered
in fur.
Lexie Saige